The New Third Act

A Woman's Guide to Midlife and Beyond

Suzanne Justice Carr, PhD

The New Third Act: A Woman's Guide to Midlife and Beyond

Copyright © 2014 by Suzanne Justice Carr, PhD

All rights reserved. No part of this book may be reproduced or transmitted in any form or by any means without written permission of the author.

Other than family members, all names and identifying characteristics of those included have been changed. Some characters are amalgamations of many. Any similarity or likeness to real people is purely accidental.

Editing, writer's coaching, and project management:
Wayne South Smith, www.waynesouthsmith.com

Cover art, interior graphics, and author photo:
Laura Nalesnik, www.mousewhiskers.com

ISBN: 978-0-692-26350-1

*To women approaching, in, or beyond midlife
who seek fulfillment, empowerment, and self-love
and want the same for other women.*

Contents

	Author's Note i
Prologue	Becoming Real 1
Part One	**The Three Acts of a Woman's Life**
	1 Past and Present 13
	2 The Upside Down Life. 17
Part Two	**Life's First and Second Acts**
	3 Learning from the Past. 31
	4 The First Act 35
	5 The Second Act 51
Part Three	**Midlife Passage**
	6 The Passage to the Third Act 61
	7 Awakening at Midlife 63
	8 Facing the Challenges of Midlife 75
	9 The Challenge of Role and Identity ... 77

10	The Challenge of the Body 91
11	The Challenge of Loss 103
12	The Challenge of Authenticity 121
13	The Third Act Choice 127

Part Four **The New Third Act**

14	The Path of Growth 133
15	Healing and Transforming 137
16	Simplifying and Strengthening 151
17	Discovering Your Inner Observer ... 165
18	Silencing the Inner Critic 175
19	Going Deeper 185
20	Claiming Our Feminine Strengths .. 195
21	Standing In Your Power 209
22	Learning from Relationships 217
23	Finding Your True Work 231

Epilogue The Call of This Moment to Be Real 241

Acknowledgements *245*

About The Author *249*

Author's Note

At my 80th birthday celebration—a celebration with live performance, food, drink, family, and friends—there were three readings from the draft of this book. After a particularly funny one involving my older brother Dick, he stood up and adamantly stated, "I don't remember that." Next, he proceeded to tell an equally funny story from *his* memory about some of my shenanigans, which, of course, I didn't remember at all. So, in front of the gathered crowd, there we were, me 80 and him 84, holding our own that our story was the true one just like two children telling their sides of "what happened" to our long-gone Mother. Everyone was entertained, and, of course, the argument remains unsettled.

Memory is individual, selective, and often fades. Still, it doesn't make the truth of one's life invalid.

I have done my best to present the truth as I know it and as I lived it within these pages. There is no formal qualitative or quantitative research completed for this book and none found to support it. There are no works cited and no research list. These are true stories about living.

This book offers the reader an opportunity to gain ideas and techniques for more fulfillment in the Third Act of life. However, please note that the information in this book is no substitute for psychological treatment. In the event you think you are suffering from any psychological condition, please seek appropriate help.

Just as I have offered to those in the therapy groups I've led, in this book I've chosen to highlight more of my own experiences as I can share them more honestly and thoroughly.

Other than family members, all names and identifying characteristics of those included have been changed. Some characters are amalgamations of many. Any similarity or likeness to real people is purely accidental.

My hope is that you, dear reader, truly *do* see yourself in this book, because the ability to relate, to witness your truth reflected from other's experiences, is the beginning of feeling grounded in society and understanding yourself.

Prologue

Becoming Real

Nothing in my life happened as expected.

One of the best things about having a life that doesn't seem to work is that you then have a chance—are often *forced*—to stand back and look at things, try to understand what went "wrong," and in the process, grow and expand your life in ways that you otherwise might not have done.

In my case, I habitually looked first at myself since I always assumed that anything that went wrong was my fault. As a strategy, that wasn't totally bad because I learned a lot, but it was incomplete. Later, when I began to look outside myself and develop a more complete picture of my life, I realized that everything wasn't my fault, that other people had problems, too, as did our society as a whole. I saw that much of what I learned about life while growing up was wrong, or, at best, inappropriate, as a basis for putting together a satisfying life. I know this is true for many other people as well. In my opinion, it's especially true for women who are often left to face adult life in a disempowered state based on unrealistic fantasies, unworkable strategies, and social roles that inhibit or prevent their personal growth.

As for myself, I don't want to imply that my life has been a bad life. It hasn't. True, I've had my share of problems, but compared to the lives of the many women whose stories I have been privileged to hear, my life has been good. It's just that I rarely felt in control of things, many of which seemed to evolve in spite of me, leaving me to cope with many unplanned, unexpected, and often difficult situations. I felt that I was living on a "survival" level, constantly forced to react to the demands of the immediate situation without a chance to keep my head above water, breathe easily, and see the big picture.

My career path is a good example. In college, I majored in music not knowing what I wanted to do with that degree, only knowing that I did *not* want to be a music teacher. So what did I become? A teacher, of course, in junior high school—my worst possible nightmare! But I survived, and from there, I lurched from one career to another. For three years I was a high school choral director, then after a year's graduate training, a junior high guidance counselor, followed by four years as a graduate student in social psychology and a nine-year stint as a professor of psychology in a women's college. Then, back to graduate school—this time in clinical psychology—after which I started my practice as a psychotherapist, helping people understand their lives and find their true paths, while, not incidentally, doing the same for myself in the process. I finally arrived at the place where I was supposed to be all along: living a happy life while working with women navigating their Third Act.

Getting here, however, has not been a straight path or an easy one. When I first told my life story to my therapist, she said, "Your whole life sounds like an accident!" In some ways, she was right. It's true that I achieved much success in my life, but it's also true that I did so without a sense of direction and with little satisfaction. On the outside, it looked great, but on the inside I felt confused, fragmented, and insecure, an imposter who could at any moment be exposed as the inadequate person I really believed myself to be. Things rarely went smoothly. For example, I received my undergraduate degree from Radcliffe, but, in the process, was forced to take two years off because of pregnancy and childbirth.

I finished my senior year with a two-year-old child in tow. Later, I completed my doctorate at Georgia State, but I did so while going through my second child's birth and infancy, thus learning to take exams with a sleeping baby on my lap. I'm proud of these achievements, but I could have attained them more easily and felt a deeper sense of ownership for them had I lived my life with more conscious intent. And I would have had I known.

The problem was that I *didn't* know. It was only after I was older and gained more insight that I was able to understand what had happened and to convert my "accidental" life into an intentional one, a *conscious journey* instead of a rambling unconscious one, a *real* life instead of a fantasy life.

My journey toward a more conscious life began in earnest when I reached midlife and was confronted with life challenges that I truly did not feel capable of handling. It began with the shock of turning fifty, followed later by successively greater shocks of sixty, seventy, and now, eighty. Then came the physical shocks from my midlife body in the form of scary symptoms involving my heart and my spine, all of which turned out to be benign for the time being, then came the life shocks—pain, losses, disappointments. One of the worst was my mother's death just as I was struggling with the aforementioned scary symptoms and a growing sense of my own mortality. And all of this came on top of starting a new career, supporting family members through life's difficulties, and experiencing the birth of my first grandchild, which was wonderful, but shocking. How could I *possibly* be a grandmother?!

There were times while I was living through all this that I felt totally overwhelmed. But gradually, I learned to deal with it. Many experiences contributed to that learning, but one experience in particular stands out in my mind. It brought me face to face with life and death in a way I had never been before.

I had only been in practice for a few years when I received a call from Terri, a colleague requesting a session with me. We had met several times professionally, and although I did not know her well, I liked her and admired her work.

At her first appointment, Terri walked into my office, sat down facing me, and said, "I have been diagnosed with ovarian cancer, and I'm terribly afraid!" She broke into sobs, and we sat for a while without words, both of us struggling—her with grief and me with shock and the urgency I felt to find words to convey my empathy. Finally, I said something like, "Terri, I'm so sorry. And of course you're afraid; everyone is." The words felt totally inadequate for the gravity of the situation, but I also knew that even though I could not verbalize it, on some deep gut level inside myself I had, in that moment, made a decision: Come what may, I wanted to be there for Terri, whatever that meant and however long it took.

That was the beginning of our three-year journey together—the last three years of Terri's life. For Terri, it was a journey filled with fear, anger, frustration, sorrow, anguish, and eventual acceptance of her death. For me, the journey was a challenge to live up to what Terri needed and I wanted to be for her, which was a source of support, nurturance, and strength, accompanying her to whatever depths of pain and despair this journey held. This meant coping with my own feelings: inadequacy to meet this challenge; guilt for living, when Terri, who was twenty years my junior, was facing her death; terror at facing the inevitable mortality of us all; and later, after her death, regrets over times when I felt I had been less than I should have been for her.

We both grew during the journey, but it was Terri who led the way. Perhaps a year before her death when her ultimate fate was increasingly real, I remember the day Terri looked at me and said, "No matter what happens, I want to be aware. I want to be real. I want to make this journey consciously." She did. And I did my best to stay with her.

One day, shortly before her death when Terri was too weak to come to my office and we had shifted our meeting place to the sunny, comfortable upstairs bedroom in her home, she said to me, "Remember our first session? Do you know why I stayed with you? It was because when I told you about my cancer you didn't leave me." It was my gut level decision that she felt; the rest didn't matter.

In the years since Terri's death, I have often reflected on my time with her. I know that our journey changed my life. From being with her, I absorbed some of her strength and became more aware of my own. I realized that if she could approach her death with full awareness, then I could do the same for my life. I knew that, like Terri, I wanted to be conscious no matter what happened. And I now felt strong enough to do that. I chose to face my life, aging and all, rather than take the easier path of denial and avoidance.

I chose to be real.

Since then, many events have tested that choice, and I haven't always passed that test. In the beginning, when faced with situations that challenged me to be real and speak my truth when it was uncomfortable to do so, I often avoided the challenge. But I found that I could no longer avoid my own awareness; I knew what I was doing, and I didn't like it. Gradually the internal pressure to be authentic with myself and others, and to do what I felt called to do in life became impossible to ignore. I was forced to face my fears and act. I suppose that's courage, although I never really felt courageous. I felt that I chose the better of two options—to act, even while shaking in my boots, often literally, or to live in the constant shame of knowing that underneath I was a coward. And most of all, I didn't want to come to the end of my life only to discover that I had never really lived.

So I stayed the course. And along the way, I discovered that becoming "real" is a *journey*, not a *destination*. It is a commitment to face life authentically day by day, in all situations, no matter how small or insignificant they may seem, and to live life every moment with intent and awareness. I also discovered an important truth: when you start down the path of awareness, you can't go back. Once opened, the door cannot be closed. And I also know that I wouldn't close that door even if I could, because I realized that living a real life, with all its pain as well as its joy, is more fulfilling by far than any false life that I lived before. And that, more than anything else, is why I say that the Third Act is the best time of my life.

I know that many women in their Third Acts have had experiences similar to mine, perhaps even had lives that up to that point felt like "accidents." And some, like me, chose to face their fears and live authentically, and like me, are surprised to find that these years have become the best of their lives. Moreover, I believe that the Third Act *should* be, *could* be, and under the right circumstances, *would* be the best part of every woman's life.

Every woman can choose to be real.

And I am not alone in this thinking. Over the past few years, I have met many other women in their Third Acts who have come to the same conclusion and are also living conscious, creative lives. Like me, they are sharing their experience with others through teaching, writing, companioning, and acting as models for other women. They are my family, my friends, my clients, my therapists, my teachers, my guides, and my support through these often difficult, but incredibly fulfilling, years. Not only have my life and my work been greatly enriched by their presence, my journey would not have been possible without them.

In the end, however, each woman's story is uniquely her own. Fulfillment, if it happens, will come through *herself*, reflecting *her* choices and *her* initiative. No one formula fits all. Moreover, finding fulfillment in the Third Act is not just for women who happen to have more education, or public success. It is for any woman who chooses to take the journey of consciousness and live an authentic life. It is a meeting with one's soul, if you will, and it can happen to any of us who choose to open to our own experience, learn from it, and discover the meaning of our own lives.

The purpose of this book is not to show you *the* way, but *a* way to find fulfillment in midlife and beyond. I will share what I've learned along the way from my own and other women's lives in the hopes that this resonates with your life and helps you discover the path to your own personal truth.

Please join me on the journey to fulfillment!

PART ONE

The Three Acts of a Woman's Life

I

Past and Present

Women's lives unfold in three acts.

The First Act, childhood, is the time we grow, learn, and prepare for life. As children, we experience ourselves as the center of the world with little awareness of what others want or feel, or what impact we may have on them. We live in the present, guided primarily by our feelings and our desires of the moment with little capacity to understand, verbalize, or much less, control them. In that sense, we live authentically but not consciously.

The Second Act is our adulthood, which I see as the years from approximately twenty to fifty. For most of us this is the time when we leave our childhood home, take on jobs and careers, form intimate relationships, marry, and have homes and children of our own. Our growing responsibilities force us to focus outside of ourselves, centering our lives on others and on the external world. The child that we once were is buried under layers of whom and what others want us to be. We become less aware of our inner experience, often not knowing what we want or feel or even who we are as a person. We may become our "roles" and lose our authenticity.

Sometime in the middle of our life, we enter the Third Act, and everything changes. Children grow up, leave home, and form their own lives. Our role as mother ends. Relationships and marriages evolve or sometimes dissolve. Our careers may end or cease to satisfy us. We are challenged to find new identities and new meaning for our lives.

Until recently, there were few roles open to older women. Those available were written long ago in a culture where women rarely lived past midlife, and if they did, they were often seen as burdens who, at best, could help with the grandchildren or otherwise keep themselves entertained with superficial activities. Mostly, older women became invisible, living quietly in the background while the younger people around them lived "real" lives.

But in the New Third Act, women have a choice. Instead of allowing ourselves to be drawn into the old cultural scripts and decline into an irrelevant old age, we can move in new directions and blaze new trails, ones that offer exciting possibilities for self-fulfillment and personal growth. With the wisdom and experience gained over the years, we can claim our power and write a new script in which we are the central characters in our own story—a story that honors the true self and gives expression to the voice within us that cries out for wholeness and authenticity. The New Third Act becomes the crowning period of our lives.

The Upside Down Life

I am a woman in my Third Act who chose to write a new script.

That choice has sent me on a journey of self-discovery and personal growth that I still travel to this day. There are times when the journey is hard and scary, when I feel confused and lonely, and when I doubt myself. But there are many more times when I am personally fulfilled and deeply joyous in ways that I never felt before. So, in the end, it has been more than worth it. I'm finally living the life I was meant to live, and in the process, I feel that I have uncovered a marvelous "secret" that I would now like to share with other women:

The Third Act can be the best time of all.

This realization first came to me on a sunny winter's day about twenty years ago when I was in my early sixties. Sitting in my study surrounded by my work, I gazed past my beloved Steinway—a childhood dream finally come true in my later years—onto the familiar tree-lined street in Atlanta that had been my home for the over forty years. Reflecting on my life over the past few years, I slowly became aware of a deep sense of contentment and gratitude flowing through my body. I had never felt anything quite like it before. "I'm happy," I thought, "*really* happy. Happier than I have ever been. This is the best time of my life!"

Let me be clear. When I say this is the *best* time, I don't mean the *easiest*. Like everyone, I experience the down sides of getting older—physical decline, low energy, losses, disappoints. But, in spite of the inevitable struggles that come in our later years, my life has become more rich, full, and satisfying than ever before. I have work that is fulfilling, a home that is warm and comfortable, and family and friends I love dearly. And best of all, somewhere along the way, I seemed to have learned to love myself. I feel complete.

Delighted as I was to discover this secret new happiness, it was definitely *not* what I had expected. Nothing in my earlier life had ever suggested that the Third Act, life in midlife and beyond, would be the best time in my life. And certainly, nobody had ever modeled such a possibility.

Quite the opposite. From my earliest childhood, I was taught the traditional view: marriage and motherhood are the pinnacles of a woman's life, and then after that, it was all downhill. Now, I realize that in my life, just the opposite happened. The years that I thought would be best were the worst, and the years I thought would be the worst have been the best.

But old beliefs die hard. So, in spite of experience to the contrary, for many years I continued to believe in the traditional view. I suspect many women of my age have similar stories. Here's mine:

When I was a little girl, my friends and I looked forward to the time when we would grow up to be "big ladies," just like our mothers. We loved playing "dress up," putting on our mothers' old clothes and high-heeled shoes, preening and hobbling around the neighborhood pretending to be beautiful ladies. We also loved being "mommy" to our baby dolls or dressing our girl dolls in their skating costumes like Sonja Henie, or fancy dresses like Shirley Temple or our other favorite movie stars. To us, being a big lady or a mommy was the high point of life, the finest role for our aspirations.

We learned this from watching our own mothers and from the many fairy tales that we were told about Prince Charming and living "happily ever after." And, at least in my case, from asking my mother endless questions about what it was like to be a grown-up woman I remember one day in particular when I overheard her telling my brother that he should be a dentist when he grew up. Curious, I asked, "Mommy, what can I be when I grow up?" And she said, "You can be a teacher or a nurse, then you will get married and have children."

From this I learned that women and men had different kinds of lives. For women, getting an education and working toward a career were simply steps toward the bigger goal of becoming a wife and mother. Being married and having children was more important than anything else. I remember being a little disappointed with this, but after all, that's what my mother had done. For four years she was a teacher, and then she got married and had children. In my unconscious, childlike way, I assumed that my mother was happy to be who she was and with how she lived her life, so I assumed that I would be happy, too.

If anybody had asked me in those days to describe a woman's life, I would probably have said something like this: First, we are little girls with mommies that take care of us. Then we grow into big girls with painted fingernails, pin-curled hair, pretty dresses, and boyfriends that take us out on "dates." We might go to college and learn to be teachers or nurses. Then, just like in fairy tales, we meet our "Prince Charming," fall in love, get married, have children, and live happily ever after.

As I got older, I realized that life was not quite so simple. I learned to see things more realistically but not as much as you might think. Even as an adult, struggling with an unhappy marriage and the conflicting demands of married life, parenthood, college, and career, I told myself that I was happy, or, if I wasn't happy at the moment, I could fix what was wrong and then I would be happy. After all, I *should* be happy—I was living in the "pinnacle of my life"—and if I wasn't, it must somehow be my fault. As far as the future was concerned, I couldn't see anything to look forward to except getting old and decrepit, or, even worse, an ugly old fairy tale witch that everybody hated.

However, when I finally arrived at midlife and entered my Third Act, I realized my view of life had been wrong. The Second Act, my adulthood, was not the pinnacle of my life, and the Third Act was not all "downhill." In fact, looking at how my whole life had unfolded, I saw that the pattern of my life was the exact opposite of what

I had been taught to believe: My life was the hardest when it should have been the best, and the best when it should have been the hardest. I had somehow managed to live an Upside Down Life.

In my mind, I see two life patterns: my life as I expected it to be, and my life as it actually happened. I labeled these two patterns the Traditional Paradigm and the Modern Paradigm.

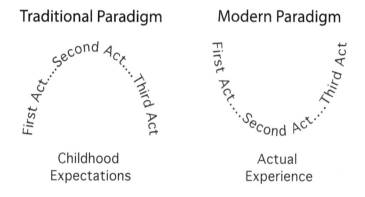

The life that I expected, the Traditional Paradigm, formed an inverted U-shape. Starting in the First Act, life got continually better, reaching its peak of happiness in the Second Act only to decline again in the Third Act.

My life as it actually happened, the Modern Paradigm, formed an opposite, perfect U-shape: In the First Act, I was happy in my childhood but grew less happy in adolescence. In the Second Act, my adulthood, I reached the depth of my unhappiness. In the Third Act, my life changed course, and I became happy again.

Of course, this picture is an over-simplification. My real life was much more complex than that; the Second Act wasn't all bad, and the Third Act hasn't been all good. But the overall pattern is true.

Seeing this pattern so clearly before me led me to wonder if other women shared my experience. Had they, too, lived Upside Down Lives? And if so, how did this happen?

One day, on a visit to Florida, I put these questions to a longtime friend and colleague. Years ago, Ann and I had emotionally supported each other through graduate school and early careers while struggling with the never-ending demands of single parenting. Now in our Third Acts and together for the first time in several years, we discovered to our surprise and delight that we both were happier than we had ever been. Although details of our lives were different, they followed the same pattern. We both had lived Upside Down Lives.

Ann and I decided to explore this pattern further. Together, we ran an informal survey, asking women to share their stories with us and rate their level of satisfaction at each stage of their lives. Our sample included fifty women, aged forty to sixty-five, with life patterns that varied: some were married, some divorced, some had children, others did not. Regardless, the results were the same: the majority rated their First and Third Acts as Very Satisfying, and their Second Act as Unsatisfying. Like Ann and me, they had lived Upside Down Lives.

Of course, what we found in our unscientific survey may not be true for all women, but from my work of 30 years focusing on women in the Third Act, I believe that it is true for many women, especially those who are currently in midlife and beyond and were exposed to the Traditional Paradigm. I wondered, "How could the pattern of so many women's lives be so different from what they were taught as children?" The answer, I think, is that although most of us grew up under the Traditional Paradigm, by the time we reached our Second Act that paradigm was no longer operative. Women's lives had changed.

For our mothers and grandmothers, the traditional view of women's lives may have accurately described the way people lived. And for many years, it was not challenged. Why should it have been? Most women did not live past fifty, and for those who did, there was little to look forward to. Women of any age were not welcome in public life, and the opinions of older women, in particular, were given little heed or respect.

But in the latter half of the twentieth century, all that began to change. A powerful women's movement swept across the country, opening doors of opportunity that had been closed to women for centuries. With the help of strong feminist leaders, women were guided to a new level of self-knowledge, self-respect, and understanding of the strength and value in the feminine view of life. In addition, women's health dramatically improved. We felt better, lived longer, and had more active, involved lives.

Now, women in midlife find themselves facing a whole new span of life—thirty to forty years for us to live as we please. We had entered a new territory, unknown to our female forebears, one with an unfamiliar landscape, many possible paths to follow, and few, if any, guideposts to show the way. We had arrived at a frontier, open to exploration, and waiting to be developed in any way we chose. We had entered the New Third Act!

Faced with these new possibilities, some women pull back. Perhaps out of habit or fear, they cling to Second Act roles, hoping to recapture the known terrain of their previous lives where the rules were clear and women who followed them were assured of having a place in the scheme of things, albeit not a very happy place. Other women, either unable or unwilling to go back to the old life or to create a new one, allowed themselves to sink into aging as defined by the Traditional Paradigm, becoming irrelevant, unnecessary, and often a burden to others, to society, and, in the end, perhaps even to themselves.

But for those of us who refuse to go back to our former lives, and yet will not accept the traditional definition of aging, there is only one option: step forward, make our own way, and create a new life in the unexplored territory in which we now find ourselves. Our life from birth wound its way down through childhood and into adult life, then turned upward to culminate in the New Third Act. There, at the pinnacle of our lives, with the broad perspective of age and experience, we can finally put it all together and see the meaning of our journey.

Looking back, we see that much of our life was spent looking outside ourselves, taking care of others, doing what we thought we *should* do rather than what we really *wanted* to do. And in the process, we often lost ourselves. Looking forward, we see the end of the tunnel and realize our lives will not go on forever. We're faced with the possibility that we could come to the end of our life without ever having really lived it! With this realization, every moment becomes precious. The hopes and dreams that we had when we were young, but later we repressed, once again come forward and demand to be recognized and fulfilled. We feel a deep longing, a desire to move forward, to do the work we are called to do, to be our true selves, to find fulfillment in our lives.

PART TWO

Life's First and Second Acts

Learning from the Past

When I began my Midlife Passage, I discovered the first step was to look back and see where I had been. I realized that the first two acts of my life set the stage for my Third Act journey. And I thought, if this were true for me, it was most likely true for other women as well. For all of us, if we are to find fulfillment in the New Third Act, we must understand the patterns that have shaped our lives to this point, where and how these patterns originated, and whether or not we want to maintain them. What is valuable and needs to be protected and nurtured? What is useless or obstructive and needs to be discarded or healed? Without this knowledge, we cannot move forward in a meaningful way.

From the perspective of the New Third Act, with the clear vision of hindsight and the wisdom of many years' experience, we can now look back at our lives and see what was not visible to us earlier in life. We can see the "raw material" of our personality and how it was shaped, sometimes advantageously and sometimes not, by the people and events in the First and Second Acts of our lives. With this awareness, we can better understand who we are and why we did what we did. We may discover qualities within ourselves that our parents did not notice, or even more damaging to us, qualities they perceived as inappropriate or just plain bad. Over the years, these qualities may become invisible to us, but when through hindsight we discover them, they may, in fact, turn out to be strengths—the strengths we need to face the challenges of midlife and bring meaning and fulfillment to us in our New Third Act.

Some may feel that they have no such resources in their childhoods. But that's not true. No matter how difficult our early years may have been, or how bleak and devoid of love and support, we always have our experiences. Even the experiences that seem insignificant, or those that are so painful we fear to revisit them, hold secrets of implanted strengths and lessons learned. Almost any experience can serve as raw material if we are willing to do the work of bringing it to consciousness and molding it into mature form.

And so, we begin our journey to the New Third Act by looking back on our lives, starting with the First Act, our childhood. To lead the way, I will share stories from my life, using key events in my childhood to show how early experiences shaped my life, both as a child and, later in my life, as an adult.

As you read these stories, I invite you to remember how your own childhood shaped your personality and affected your life. Ponder the questions at the end of each chapter. Meditate on them; write in a journal; share with a trusted friend or group of confidantes; or follow your intuition to the best method. Allow yourself to open up to the feelings these memories engender in you, so you can better understand your life, and through this understanding, build a meaningful, fulfilling New Third Act.

4
The First Act

I was born September 29, 1933, in Portsmouth, a small town in southern Ohio. Both of my parents came from poor families in eastern Ohio.

My mother grew up on a farm with her parents and five siblings in a log house that her father built. She idolized her father, and because of his encouragement, she worked hard in school, graduated first in her class, and went on to "normal school," a college for teachers. She was the only one of the family that went beyond high school.

Starting when she was only eighteen years old, my mother taught for four years in a one-room country school. When I was a child, I loved to hear her tell about her challenges as a teacher, like the time she faced down the class bully and sent him home after he broke the handle off the outdoor water pump—their only source of drinking water—or her adventures riding to and from her work every day on a rascally old horse named "Buddy."

I knew less about my father's childhood, and what I heard sounded grim. As a young boy, he walked miles to school each day, arriving early so he could fire up the stove before others arrived. Then, at age eleven, he was forced to quit school and work in the coal mines with his father and brother. He was drafted in World War I and sent to France where he worked as a machine gunner's mate at a time when the average life of a machine gunner was fleeting. Luckily, he survived uninjured except for the loss of his teeth from exposure to poison gas. After the war, he tried to get more education with little success and gave up when his mother threw away all his mail-ordered books because she didn't trust "book learnin'." Eventually, he became a manager of a Kroger grocery store where he remained for the rest of his working life.

My parents were married in the summer of 1929. Three months later, the stock market crashed, plunging the country into a deep depression. Through hard work and careful management, my parents got us through the depression well enough, even managing to buy a house for four thousand dollars—all the money they had in the world. For the next twelve years, that house was our home.

My memories start in that house on a beautiful little street called Cypress Street. This house and this street are central to my life because they set the stage for my early experiences, which in turn shaped my personality and the patterns of my life. Some of the experiences were positive, helping me to build and express my natural strengths, but others had the opposite effect, sapping my strength and undermining my confidence and self-esteem. Following are two such stories from my childhood.

Gifts Of My Childhood

From the summer before I was two years old, I had the complete run of Cypress Street. It wasn't supposed to be that way. My mother had, in fact, planned for me to play in the lovely little fenced play space she built in the back yard. But from the moment she put me in my play yard, all I did was stand at the gate and scream. So, to save her sanity, she opened the gate and let me run free.

And run free I did. Throughout the years of my childhood through age 11, Cypress Street was my kingdom.

The New Third Act

Every day, weather permitting, I roamed up and down the street exploring my domain. By the time I was four or five years old, I knew every house, yard, and garden; every crack in the sidewalk and bump in the red brick street; and every tree, path, and hiding place in the surrounding woods and fields. I also knew everybody who lived on the street—all the adults and children, as well as all cats and dogs, who, like the humans, were considered by all to be residents of Cypress Street.

I was allowed to run, climb, and play with both boys and girls in any way I liked. Sometimes I was a cowboy, a mounted policeman, a wild Indian, or a soldier. Or other times, when I felt more "little girlish," I played dolls, paper dolls, or make-believe games where we could "'tend like" we were anything we wanted to be—mommies, teachers, or even movie stars like Sonja Henie or Shirley Temple.

Sometimes, though, I just wanted to be by myself and think my own thoughts. My mother usually found me on the back porch lost in my thoughts, or as she called it, daydreaming. She thought it was a waste of time, but for me it was peaceful to go deep within myself and create my own inner world. I felt free to imagine whatever I wished and to explore any idea that appealed to me.

The First Act

Often on my daily wanderings up and down Cypress Street, I would drop in to visit a neighbor, chat for a while, and maybe stay for lunch. My favorite neighbor was my mother's best friend, a woman known to everyone—adult or child—simply as "Billie." As a young child, I spent many happy hours with Billie in her kitchen, watching as she did her chores, like ironing the family's clothes or baking one of her famous angel food cakes—I always got to lick the bowl—all the while enchanting me with stories from her childhood. On really special days Billie would allow me to play her beautiful spinet piano with the glass tear-drop ornaments that sat on each side of the keyboard, twinkling in the morning sunlight. I would ask politely, "Billie, may I play your piano?" And she would reply, "Yes, if you wash your hands first." I would run upstairs, wash my hands, run back down, plunk myself on the piano bench and place my hands on the keyboard, my five-year-old legs dangling below still unable to reach the pedals.

I loved that piano, the feel of the smooth black and white keys under my fingers, and the beautiful sound they made when I pressed the keys. Experimenting with different sounds, I would run my hands all over the keyboard from treble to bass, sometimes singing along as I played. I created what I thought of as "my music." Billie thought of it that way, too. She listened as she did her chores, from time to time giving me supportive "oohs" and "aahs," and when I was finished, she always told me how beautiful it was and thanked me for my concert.

When I wasn't visiting neighbors, playing with friends, or daydreaming on my own, I could usually be found doing my most favorite thing in the whole world—climbing trees. Among my peers, male or female, I was the unquestioned champion tree-climber. Climbing was natural for me. When I was climbing, I felt powerful, strong, and confident. I always knew what branches to hold and where to put my feet, and in all my years of climbing, I never fell. My success at climbing planted a seed of self-confidence that, at some level, stayed with me over the years.

As time went by, I came to know every tree on Cypress Street and all the neighboring areas as well. And those that were climbable, I knew limb by limb. But my favorite tree, by far, was the majestic sycamore that stood in Billie's side yard. Its bark was smooth, its branches perfectly spaced for my 4'2" body, and when I climbed to the top, which I always did, it was exactly the right height for viewing my Cypress Street kingdom. I loved the feeling of being at the top of the tree, swaying in the wind

The First Act

with the warm morning sun on my face. There, in my own private world, I could think my thoughts and dream my dreams, and nobody would disturb me. I knew that I had a special relationship with that sycamore tree, and I was sure that the tree felt the same way.

Then one day, for reasons only "big people" could understand, some men came and cut the top out of my beloved tree. They sliced off its beautiful head, leaving it looking ravaged and deformed! At first I was horrified and deeply grieved, but then I made a discovery. When I climbed my tree to explore its damage, I realized that the slashed-off top of the trunk had become a perfect seat for me—my personal throne—where I could view my kingdom and daydream to my heart's delight. It was as if the tree's new shape had been made just for me. I no longer cared why the "big people" had done this to my tree. The tree didn't seem to mind, and I had a gift that I enjoyed for many years of my childhood.

Looking back on my life from my current perspective, I reflect upon the childhood gifts illustrated in this story. The first thing that comes to mind is freedom, a gift from my mother when she opened the gate and let me run free. I've never forgotten that feeling of freedom to explore, both in the world around me, and in my thoughts and imagination. Another gift was never being confined to the limiting script of "being a lady." I was never discouraged from playing "cowboy" by being told I had to be a "cowgirl." No one indicated that there weren't any female Canadian Mounties. I was allowed free will in my imagination and choice to be any role I felt suited me.

For a while, when I was an adult smothered by the responsibilities of family and career, I lost contact with that feeling of freedom. But as I moved into my Third Act, it returned, filling me once again with a craving to explore, to make up for what I had missed during my adult years, and to live my life with the gusto and fullness of my childhood years.

I think that all of us have our special "angels" in our lives, and Billie was one of mine. She gave me something that I needed as a child but could not get from my own mother. Even though my mother gave me freedom, Billie was gentle and sweet in ways that my mother was not. She gave me her attention and took my questions and childish performances seriously. She made me feel special in ways that my mother did not. When Billie listened to my music, I was the "apple of her eye," something I rarely felt in my own family. She fed my love for stories by patiently telling, over and over, the stories from her childhood. And most of all, Billie fed my need for intimacy, for being close to other people and understanding how they felt and what went on inside their minds.

Later in my life, I often looked back fondly on those times with Billie and appreciated them anew for the part they played in implanting a core of strength and self-esteem that would help see me through the difficult times that we all face in our lives. And even now, as I sit in my study writing these words looking up occasionally at my very own piano, I wonder how much of what I have today—my life-long love of music, my close relationship with family and friends, and my work as a psychologist— had its beginning in those precious hours with Billie. It seemed so small at the time, but now I believe it's those little things that really matter.

Many years after last seeing her, Billie wrote to me after her husband died. In the letter, she referred to me as "a precious little girl," and, notwithstanding my fifty some years and the grey in my hair, I cried. My inner "little girl," who was still alive and well, needed to hear that. If Billie thought I was precious, maybe I really was. Once again, I felt like that special little girl who made beautiful music that Billie loved, and something within me softened. My heart opened to a warm flow of love for myself and for the world.

And, of course, there's the gift of the sycamore tree. Long after my old sycamore tree was gone, a victim of the post-World War II housing boom, and I had moved on to my adult life, the memory of that tree and the hours spent at its summit remained with me as a valuable gift. I remember the trust that I felt in my body, and my self-confidence, determination, and drive as I climbed, limb by limb, to the top of the tree. And I remember the sense of accomplishment and power I experienced when I reached the top and sat on my sycamore throne. Now at those times in life when it all seems too much, I can relax, close my eyes, meditate, and once again become that little girl sitting at the top of her sycamore tree happily dreaming her dreams and viewing her domain. And once again I can feel the peace of those long ago sunlit mornings on Cypress Street.

Flawed At the Core

Even though many childhood experiences gave me joy and helped me build my strengths, other experiences weakened me and left me unhappy. My mother was central to both of these experiences—the mother that opened the gate to freedom and growth also led me to believe that I was flawed.

The First Act

I became aware of the flaw because my mother pointed it out to me many times in her own "special" way that mothers have—her private code that only she and I understood. Sometimes she would say, "Sue, I'd be ashamed!" Those words alone would stop me in my tracks. But what was even worse was the look that often accompanied them—the look in her eyes that said she saw something really bad in me, something that filled her with anger and disgust, the look that had the power to fill me with disgrace.

And that was not all. Not only did my mother pronounce my "mortal sin" to the world, she cut me off from my salvation, which was her love. She turned her back on me and refused to speak, much less smile or touch, until I had redeemed myself through apologizing, pleading, and atoning for my sins—if I knew what they were.

But there was never total redemption. Shame is not something that one takes back or makes up for. Shame is an acknowledgment of something that "is," a part of oneself that, on its face, is inadequate or unacceptable. And as a child, it never occurred to me to question the truth of anything that my mother said; I accepted her pronouncements, good or bad, as a given. So each time my mother said the "shame words," I grew more convinced that I was flawed, a disappointment to my mother, and, what's worse, there was little or nothing I could do about it. My "flaw" had been revealed. All I could do was try to hide it, pray that it would go away, or if not, hope that no one would notice.

Over the years, largely through my mother's eyes, I saw many flaws in myself, and each one filled me with shame. Of course, there was the major flaw of being a girl instead of a boy like my brother Dick, and, as a girl, not being pretty like my friend, Peggie. But there were other flaws as well. One that seemed to bother my mother above all others was my undeniable need to connect with other people, to be close, and to have them like me. From a story she told me, I knew that this was an inborn need—a "flaw" at birth, if you will—and that my mother saw it as a weakness.

My mother shared that during our two weeks in the hospital, I was kept in a nursery, while she rested in a room of her own. Periodically, I was brought to her to nurse and to visit, or as we would say now, to bond. It was on one of these visits that my mother discovered how much I needed closeness and physical contact. As she told it, after feeding me she would place me in the bed beside her where we would nap side-by-side, touching each other the whole time. Then one day, my mother shifted her position so that she was no longer touching me and, to her surprise, saw me wiggle my little body toward her until I was touching her. She thought this was cute and funny and began to make a little game of it; she would intentionally move slightly away from me, and then watch me scoot toward her until we touched somewhere, even if it was just the tip of my head against her arm. Only then would I settle back into my satisfied sleep.

As a child, every time my mother told me that story, I felt sad and hurt. I was confused by my feelings because it was a cute little story, or seemed as if it should be, but it always aroused conflicted feelings in me that I didn't understand and couldn't put into words. I sensed an undertone that made me uncomfortable and left me with a feeling of humiliation. I didn't fully understand it at the time, but now I think that, consciously or unconsciously, my mother saw my need for closeness as a shameful weakness that she needed to deny, both in herself and in me.

As I grew older, my mother used my need for closeness to manipulate and control me. The manipulation was extremely powerful. When she was displeased with me, she would simply withdraw from me, refuse to talk, turn her back, and go on with her work as if I no longer existed. I can still remember those moments when, cut off from the connection I needed, I stood looking at her back, feeling desperate and alone. Sometimes I tried to hold my ground and defend what I had done, but it never worked. She had more power; she was the mother and I was the child. The ending was always the same: I would cave in, say that I was sorry, and be brought back into her good graces. And when she was ready—but not before—she would finally soften and let me back into her world. By that time, I was so grateful that I forgave her everything. Never mind my humiliation and shame. I had regained the contact I needed to survive.

Later, when I was older and had studied psychology, I learned that my mother's method of controlling me is called "withdrawal of love." In a perfect example of unintended consequences, my mother's use of withdrawal of love not only failed to weaken my need for connection; it actually strengthened it. And over time, that need generalized to other people and situations. It became difficult, sometimes impossible, for me to tolerate anger in a relationship or to maintain a disagreement with a friend without trying to make it up or cover it over in some way. I was usually the one to apologize, so I would be taken back into the magical place of connection where I was once again acceptable and all was right with the world. I became a "people pleaser."

The First Act

The ultimate irony is that, having "trained" me to please people, my mother criticized this behavior when she saw it in my other relationships. "Stick up for yourself," she would say. "You always let other people take advantage of you." Later, when my tendency to please others led me into a bad marriage, she criticized me, saying, "Why do you let him treat you like this? We didn't bring you up to live like this." And every time she talked to me like that, I felt deep shame. I believed she was right. I *should* stick up for myself. She did; other people did. But I couldn't.

Over the years, my need to connect with people continued to grow. And my feelings of shame grew right along with them. I did not trust my own perceptions. In fact, I was so focused on others that I often did not know what I really thought or felt. And if I knew, I was afraid to speak up or express an opinion for fear that what I had to offer would be seen as useless or stupid. When I was in a group or class, I was reluctant to ask a question, especially if it was not a group I knew. Performing or speaking in public became almost impossible for me. I was trapped in a cycle that I felt powerless to stop, a cycle that perpetuated into my teens and my adult years, undermining my personal power and creating many painful situations throughout my life.

Later in life, I became more aware of the negative impact my mother's message had on me. I saw how it undermined my natural strengths and deprived me of the opportunity to enjoy and expand my life in ways I was capable of doing. I was no longer willing to tolerate living my life that way. I was no longer a people pleaser.

My midlife awakening had begun.

Reflect:

What were the life circumstances of your parents before marriage, during your youth, and beyond?

What are your memories of an early childhood home—characteristics, neighborhood, friends, family interactions, pets, etc.?

Remember a positive and a negative experience from your childhood years. What did each illustrate about your life? What does it show now about how you interact with self and others? How does the reflection on the experience make you feel now in contrast to how you viewed it in the past?

The Second Act

I enjoy exchanging emails with my niece. When I first talked to her about my book, she was in her early forties with three young daughters, a husband, a home, a part-time job, and a garden she loved to work in when she has time. After reading my description of the stages of women's lives, she wrote, "I can see I'm a 'Woman in the Second Act' of life, which is subtitled 'It's Not About You.' What I have trouble with is juggling it all—motherhood, marriage, work, myself. I always 'drop the myself ball' because it's the only one I can let go of."

Laughing to myself, I thought, *What a perfect description of the Second Act of women's lives.* So, I responded "Well, I am in the Third Act, and its subtitle is 'It's all about me.'"

Women's lives in the Second Act are often heavily weighted toward the external world. This forces us to ignore, cut off, or repress large portions of our psyches—mind, soul, and spirit—and to detach from our inner lives—emotions, thoughts, and intuition. We may take our bodies for granted, turning all our energy outward. We look outside ourselves for guidance, to see who we are—or ought to be.

In our early years as adults, we are taught our value lies in sexual attractiveness as defined by the culture. In an attempt to meet the current standard for beauty, we often abuse and neglect our "imperfect" bodies. This not only damages our health, but also leaves us even more frustrated and despairing of getting the intimate, loving relationship that we desire. In addition, the neglect of our bodies cuts off the connection to our inner wisdom which resides in our bodies.

Later, our roles as wives, partners, career women, and especially as mothers, forces us to continue focusing outside ourselves. In addition to running the home, taking care of the children, and, in many cases, holding down a job, we are also the source of comfort and nurturance to others, holding everything together and seeing that everyone's needs are met. In many cases, women are also the ones who manage the finances and make the major decisions for the family. Our responsibilities are numerous and varied, requiring us to be constantly alert and aware.

Like childhood, the Second Act has both gifts and challenges. The gifts include finding a partner to share our lives, the magical experience of giving birth to another human being, creating a family of our own, caring for our children as we watch them grow into adulthood, and, for many of us, engaging in satisfying work, perhaps even a vocation or calling.

However, the challenges of the Second Act can be formidable: breaking apart of relationships that had begun with so much promise; watching our children grow into adults that are less than or different from what we hoped they would be; dealing with unexpected job loss or the failure of our career to manifest in ways we had envisioned; constantly struggling to keep up the pace demanded of us by our many responsibilities with little time for rest, leisure, or attending to our own needs; and, for many of us, throughout it all, a vague sense that our lives are not what they are "supposed to be," that somehow we have missed the boat that others seem to have found, but we don't know what is the cause or who is to blame, much less how to fix it.

In the face of all this, one wonders why we would ever choose such a life. The fact is that we have little choice in the matter. Everybody grows up. At some point, be it high school or college graduation, some unexpected event, or simply our own inner urge to fly on our own, we find ourselves moving out of our childhood nest into the adult world. There, as young women, we are confronted with the tasks that both our biology and our culture draw us to: finding a suitable mate, birthing and rearing children, and, increasingly for modern women, launching a career and learning how to financially support ourselves.

Some women have the good fortune of feeling ready. Securely supported by understanding parents or other positive circumstances, they are prepared for adult life with a solid sense of grounding within themselves, appropriate education and training, and social skills to help them maneuver successfully in the world. Thus equipped, they make the transition at a pace they can absorb, intentionally selecting the steps they will take and when they will take them.

Others of us, perhaps the majority, are less fortunate, finding ourselves thrown into the fray long before we feel ready to manage it. But once there, we cannot choose to go back. The demands of the Second Act are too present, too insistent to be ignored. For the unprepared woman, the Second Act is a harrowing process. I consider myself one of the "less fortunate" majority.

In the first years of my Second Act, I often felt uncomfortable and unhappy with my marriage and work, and I lacked confidence. I simply wondered if something was wrong with me, or maybe it was normal and everybody felt this and just lived with it better than I did. I later learned I had experienced chronic anxiety.

In addition to these struggles, my Second Act began with one of those unexpected, unplanned events: the birth of my first son. I was an immature twenty-one, not yet finished with college and not ready to take on the complex responsibilities of adult life, especially those associated with parenthood. I did take it on, but, even though I loved my son, I was often unhappy with my life at that time. I felt a big disconnect between what women were supposed to feel about pregnancy, childbirth, and mothering and what I actually felt. I thought there was something wrong with me. And in addition throughout my Second Act, I felt as though I was constantly trying to catch up with my life, always a step behind what was actually happening.

For the next thirty years of my Second Act while I dealt as best I could with school, career, marriage, and motherhood—all happening simultaneously—I lived in "survival mode." Constantly busy with my many responsibilities, fragmented and pulled from home to school to work and back again, worried and stressed over what was happening and what I imagined might happen, focused on the needs of others and the demands of the external world, I lost touch with myself. Somewhere back behind all the achieving and doing of my Second Act, there was a real person who knew what she felt and what she wanted. But I had lost touch with that person. I had almost completely transformed into the roles I was playing.

But regardless of how one moves through the Second Act, life confronts us all with the same issues. The powerful demands of the Second Act pull us so completely into the roles that we are required to play that we can hardly imagine life being otherwise. For some, these roles offer satisfaction. But in any case, whether we are happy or not, sometimes it is just easier to give in, go with the flow, allow our roles to define us, and consciously or unconsciously put our own lives on hold.

Later, when my Second Act drew to an end and I began to move into my Third Act, I found myself letting go of the roles I had played for the last twenty to thirty years and allowing the "real person" to emerge and begin the "real" life I had lost contact with many years ago.

 Reflect:

What were the gifts of your Second Act? What were the challenges?

What roles did you play in your Second Act?

What were some parts of yourself you let go of, parts that went unfulfilled?

PART THREE

Midlife Passage

The Passage to the Third Act

Women experience two major passages in their lives.

The first passage, our teen years, begins with puberty. This period of life has been widely studied and is viewed as the essential step from childhood to womanhood and all the potential fullness that adult life can offer. This is where we move from the First Act into the Second Act.

The Midlife Passage, which spans roughly the period from age forty to age sixty, centers around menopause but extends far beyond it in its meaning for life. Sadly, the Midlife Passage is generally less well understood and less valued than the puberty passage, but this time is key to vitality as we age from the Second Act to the Third Act.

In my work with women and in my own life, I have come to realize that midlife is a time of seismic changes in a woman's consciousness and sense of reality. Midlife can shatter our old identities in frightening and confusing ways, but it can also open the door to power, wisdom, and new possibilities for living. The extent of these changes has not been fully recognized and supported by most women.

The Midlife Passage is often seen as an unhappy time, full of pain and loss, leading toward the bleak, dreaded period known as "old age." And because of the many changes that are necessary in this transition, midlife tends to be turbulent and difficult. But in spite of the pain, midlife can be, and often is, very rewarding. Midlife is the time when we begin to awaken from the long "trance" of our Second Act, face challenges of a new and different kind, and make the choices that determine how we will live the rest of our lives. The deep significance of these three events—awakening to our consciousness, facing inevitable and difficult challenges, and making important choices—requires that we take a close look at each.

7

Awakening at Midlife

Like many young girls, one of my greatest childhood satisfactions was to lose myself in the world of fairy tales. The ones I loved best were those in which a young woman, often presented as a princess, falls into some dire mishap from which she is eventually rescued by a brave young prince. Although I did not realize it at the time, these tales often conveyed powerful, underlying messages to little girls about how they should live their lives and what they can expect in the future.

"Sleeping Beauty" is one of these tales. The story is familiar to most of us: A beautiful young princess, who is placed under a curse at birth by a wicked witch, pricks her finger on a spindle and falls into a deep, one-hundred-year sleep. Many years later, a prince from a neighboring kingdom hears of her plight, fights his way through the overgrown thorns around her castle, and finds the sleeping princess. He is so overcome by her beauty that he kneels down and kisses her. Immediately the spell is broken and Sleeping Beauty awakes. In a joyous ceremony, they are married, and the prince carries her off to his kingdom where they live happily ever after.

As a child, I heard the message of this tale this way: *Someday when I grow up, the man who truly loves me will find me, and through him, I will awaken to my real life. Meeting that man is the crucial event of my life. Nothing that happens before that is important.* I believed this message because it fit perfectly with what I had been taught—the traditional role of a woman as wife and mother was what every woman dreamed of, and this was the life that would bring every woman lasting happiness. I think that's the message the tale intended to convey and the one that most little girls heard.

But now, many years later, I believe the true message of the tale should be: *The kiss of the prince will not wake you up; it will put you to sleep. Only later, after living through the realities of life, will you truly awaken, this time to your own self and the life that you were meant to live.* In other words, the tale had it completely backwards, leaving many women deeply severed from their authentic selves, attempting to live a real life based on a fantasy that never was and never will be.

Sometime during our adolescent years, influenced by what our mothers told us and by the cultural myths to which we were all exposed, women fall into a trance. In this state, we sleepwalk through our lives, living the roles that are given to us, pretending that we are happy and all is as it should be as we try hard not to notice anything that suggests otherwise. Finally, twenty to thirty years later when the problems pile up, becoming too overwhelming to ignore, we awaken. The spell of the prince's kiss is finally broken. By then, we are in midlife, facing realities that we have spent long years and much effort trying to avoid. Jolted out of our trance, we may at first feel lost and overwhelmed. But gradually, we may also realize that we are now free, free to be our true selves and reclaim the life we left behind many years ago.

In "Sleeping Beauty," the kiss is a metaphor for sexual awakening that occurs in adolescence. But it is a false awakening. The onset of sexuality leads us to believe that we are finally grown up, coming into the prime of our lives. We are free to do as we please, believing in the absolute inevitability of our "happily ever after" ending. We discover in later years that this is a delusion. Instead of true awakening, we are led into a trance, one that deprives us of the full use of our natural intuition, sometimes even our rational minds, leaving us to the mercy of our hormones and daydreams. We are left to lead unconscious lives.

All of this is quite ironic when you consider that puberty, the adolescent event that brings a girl physically and emotionally into womanhood, actually deprives her of her full power as a woman. The awakening of sexuality pulls her into the roles of wife and mother, roles that strongly encourage passivity, dependence, and enmeshment in the lives of others. Women are taught to focus their awareness outside themselves and to look toward the outside world—especially the male world—for validation and direction. In the process, they lose their connection to the inner self, the core of their being, and the source of their personal power. Often, this power is regained at menopause, the midlife event that leads a woman to a renewed connection to self.

This loss of power during the years of early adulthood has serious consequences for women. Unlike Sleeping Beauty, real women do not have the luxury of lying in a royal bed for one hundred years waiting for the prince to arrive and take charge of her life. For a real woman, life goes right on happening in spite of her trancelike state. Education, career, marriage, motherhood, and all the rest demand her utmost attention, often at the same time. And Prince Charming, when and if he does arrive, is never the hero/savior we imagined he would be. The bottom line is that our hopeful "sleeping beauty," like everyone else in the world, is often left to deal with life on her own without her full power at her disposal and no solid ground of being on which to stand. Lacking confidence and self-direction, she is conflicted and fragmented by the many external demands placed on her. Trance or no trance, she still must solve the problems of real life.

For some women, the trance is never complete. In this case, there is a part of the self—the core of our being—that never goes along with the Prince Charming dream. The more perceptive we are, the more capable we are of self-reflection, and the more our core resists. In this case, a split occurs in the personality: part of the woman sinks into the dream while another part stays on the course of self-growth This split is destructive to a woman's development because it divides her energy between trance and reality, leaving the growing part of the self to deal with the real world without its full strength. It is left to the true awakening at midlife to restore the wholeness that was lost at adolescence.

Perhaps I feel this so deeply because it describes my own life. Caught up in the Sleeping Beauty fantasy,

The New Third Act

but nevertheless unwilling to give up my own dreams for personal growth and achievement, I was constantly torn and conflicted. I wanted to be the Princess who was loved by the Prince, but I was unwilling to give up my own goals and ambitions. I was unable to fully commit to either. Needless to say, my life rarely went smoothly.

It's true that I achieved much success, but it's also true that I did so without a clear sense of direction and often with little satisfaction. On the outside, it all looked good, but on the inside I felt that I was lurching from one career to another confused, fragmented, and insecure, an imposter who could at any moment be exposed as the inadequate person I really believed myself to be. In my role as mother, I felt the same. I was never able to fully commit myself to mothering and never felt that I had done it right. My attention was always divided between family and career.

When my therapist told me, "Your whole life sounds like an accident," in some ways, she was right. However, seen through the retrospective lens of my Third Act where the whole pattern is evident, my life no longer seemed like an accident. In fact, given where my head was at the time, it seemed inevitable.

My brother always told me I was driven. And I think he's right, but perhaps not in the way he meant it—as a neurotic drive to compete and achieve—although that may have been a part of the picture. What feels more real to me is that I was lost and trying to find myself. I felt driven by an inner force, not to compete with others, but to become the person I was meant to be, to offer to the world whatever gifts were mine to give. But because I spent much of my early adulthood in a trance, confused between my Sleeping Beauty fantasy and my real life, and torn between family, education, and career, I was never able to fully reach that goal. Finally at midlife, I awoke from the trance and began to move forward. But it was not the kiss of the Prince that awakened me. It was real life, with all its pains, joys, and complexities.

What, then, is a "true" awakening, and why does it occur at midlife? A true awakening is a coming to consciousness, a moment when we open our eyes, both metaphorically and physically, see what is happening around us and to us, and become aware of how we, ourselves, feel about it. It is like suddenly standing on our own legs, staring into the fish tank that we formerly took to be reality. From this detached, objective perspective, we see the big picture. And for the first time, we really "get it," perhaps asking ourselves why we had ever agreed to live in such a way. It's the moment when we slap ourselves on the side of the face and say, "Duh! What was I thinking?"

It's true that throughout our lives we all have some moments like this—"wake-up calls." And perhaps we actually have partial awakenings. But, until we have the perspective that only years of experience can bring us, our awakening is likely to be incomplete.

I can easily point to a couple of instances in my own life that illustrate this point. My first marriage is an excellent example. I thought I was marrying Prince Charming, but he turned out to be Bluebeard. What did I learn from this? Not much. I did learn to view my own judgment with suspicion, but I didn't learn the crucial fact that Prince Charming is a myth. Unlearning that took many more years and much more pain.

Then there was that "little stroke" I had when I was in my early thirties and a graduate student. At the time I was struggling with a difficult curriculum, a part-time job, a new marriage, and parenting an adolescent son. Then one night, after playing tennis in the hot sun, I awoke with the worst headache I had ever experienced—and I had had plenty of them. My husband hauled himself out of bed and dragged me, sick as a dog and screaming in pain, to the ER where I was diagnosed with a hemorrhagic stroke. I spent three horrible days undergoing painful tests to confirm the diagnosis. Results showed that the stroke had been mild. A small blood vessel had burst but had healed itself, and luckily, I was left with no lasting effects.

And what did I learn from this? Considering the potentially dire consequences, very little. I did learn not to play tennis in the midday heat of a summer day. But I didn't learn the bigger lesson—that I had had a serious threat to my life, mostly because I was over-stressed, and that I needed to change some things in my life. At some level, I knew this was true, but I was still living in my fairy tale trance and wasn't yet ready to absorb that reality. The stroke was a "wake-up call" I chose to ignore.

One thing I knew for sure: if I had had that stroke later in my life, like in my Third Act, I would not have ignored it. For most us, by the time we reach midlife, the accumulation of disasters and head-on crashes with reality has piled up to the point that we can no longer ignore them. Our capacity for denial is stretched beyond its limits, plus our energy for coping with life's "slings and arrows" is badly drained. It becomes increasingly difficult to avoid seeing the reality of our life and, hopefully, our part in creating that reality. Our old allies—denial, avoidance, and rationalization—no longer work their magic. We see through our own smoke screens and recognize that the only person who was present in all of our catastrophes was our self. So, if anything is to change, we will need to be the ones doing the changing—of ourselves, our choices, and the way we live our lives. In other words, like it or not, we become more conscious. Whether we remain that way or not is up to us, but none of us can avoid a brush with this experience.

Moreover, our perspective on life is different. Years of living—and, hopefully, learning—have given us an opportunity to broaden that perspective. Of course, some of us don't take that opportunity, choosing instead to close down our minds and draw in the limits of our world view. But for those who do, we see things on a larger scale and get the big picture that we did not have before. We also understand life on a deeper level than we did in the past, leading us to see the nuances and complexities of life that we previously would have missed.

This expansion of perspective allows each of us to have a broader view of our own life. We can relive our own lives, be any age we want to be, but with a perspective that was not available to us at the time.

Sometimes I imagine myself sitting high on a mountain looking down at all the stages in life that came before the Third Act. From this perspective, I watch women in those stages struggling with many of the problems I encountered at their age, often making the same self-defeating choices I made at that age. I know they are doing the best they can, but I also know many of their decisions will have negative outcomes. From my position higher on the mountain, I can see what they cannot see. I know that at this point in my life faced with those same problems, I would make different, probably better, choices. But I don't blame them; I understand. I was there once myself. My new perspective not only gives me a broader view, it also gives me more compassion for other women and for the young woman that I once was.

Finally, one of the most important changes at this time of life is that we become aware of our mortality. When we reach our later years, we can all see the end of the tunnel, and that makes a big difference. Rationally, we always understood that the end was there, but now we really *know* it. Having lived through fifty years or more of all that life can throw at us, we no longer feel invulnerable to the vicissitudes of life. We realize that all of those terrible things that we read about and hear about, those things that we always thought of as happening to "other people" can happen to us. In fact, in one form or another, they *have* happened to us, or, if not, they *will* happen to us. Eventually we, too, will take our place among the obituaries that we've glanced at over the years. It's a very humbling and yet somehow comforting experience to realize that we're not immortal after all; we're human just like everybody else. Finally, we can "get over ourselves" and get on with living.

With increased consciousness, broader perspective, and awareness of mortality, we are not the same person we were in our twenties, thirties, or even our forties. So, when the wake-up calls come in midlife, we experience these challenges differently.

Reflect

What fairy tale or fantasy role model did you resonate with as a young girl? When did the fantasy disappear, and how did you deal with newfound reality?

When did you truly awaken in midlife? What was your true "kiss," the catalyst that brought you into reality? What did you learn, and did you retain this lesson?

Are you aware of your mortality? Does this make living your life easier or more stressful?

8

Facing the Challenges of Midlife

When we reach midlife, we encounter challenges that jar us out of our old reality and affect us at the very core of our being. When we least expect it, we may find ourselves facing challenges of gut-wrenching and life-changing proportions. We soon find that coping with these challenges requires a new kind of strength, one that forces us to reach deep inside ourselves for all the resources we can muster.

Midlife challenges come in many forms. First, there are the challenges to the roles that we played in the Second Act and the identity we built around them. The challenges may not come in the way the stories tell us, but with the dreaded words, "I want a divorce." And suddenly, we are no longer a "wife." Or they may come when we realize that our children, to whom we have devoted the last twenty or thirty years of our lives, are grown up, on their own, and no longer need us in the role of "mother."

Other challenges may come through our bodies in the form of illness, injury, disability, or the gradual decline that comes with aging. And at some point, we are also forced to face the inevitable losses of people whom we love—good friends, parents, a spouse, or even a child. Life as we knew it breaks apart, never to be the same again.

Finally, midlife confronts us all with the challenge of how to live the last third of our lives. How can we reclaim the authenticity we once experienced as a child? How can we bring meaning to our lives in the face of a culture that defines the latter part of life as a time of loss of meaning?

Difficult as it may be, it is extremely important that we consciously face these challenges as they come into our lives. Our response to them determines the direction of our lives from here on out.

9

The Challenge of Role and Identity

In the Second Act, women's lives are shaped from the "outside-in," but in the New Third Act this must be reversed. We must learn to shape our lives from the "inside-out" to find meaning. Through courage, hard work, and honest introspection, we sort ourselves from the many roles we have played in our Second Act and find our way back to the authentic person underneath. Only then can we re-experience the authenticity we once knew unconsciously as a child but which now, overlaid with years of experience, can be known consciously, and as such, it can become fodder for deeper, wiser versions of ourselves.

For many women, the hardest challenge comes in our roles as wives and mothers. The more that we have identified with these roles—seeing ourselves only as "Mrs. So-and-So" or "Mother of So-and-So"—the more difficult it will be to let go of them and reclaim our authentic selves. Let's look now at the challenges we face as we move out of these roles and how two women dealt with these challenges.

Spouse

People react in different ways to discouragement and disillusion in their marriages. Some, fearing to upset the apple cart and finding ourselves forced to face what we don't feel ready to face, choose to deny the problem. We sink into the same old marriages we've seen so much of. Maybe we relive our parent's marriage or the marriages of many of friends and relatives who chose to live unconscious lives. If we make this choice, we are forced to shut ourselves down and limit our possibilities—not a very appealing option, but it's our trade-off for ease and safety.

When faced with this issue, others respond by accepting the challenge and working on our marriages. Our relationships must change, and *we* must change to bring the relationship into alignment with the reality of

The Challenge of Role and Identity

our lives. We may go into counseling—both for ourselves and our marriages—as well as attend marriage retreats, and do plenty of deep soul-searching. This is a challenging and rocky road, but if both partners are willing, it can lead to a satisfying relationship. And in the process, we will also grow personally, which will enrich all aspects of our lives.

Sometimes, for many reasons, we are forced to face the reality that our marriage is not repairable and must end. Following is a story of one such marriage:

Carol grew up in a family that believed in doing everything right. As the oldest child of an alcoholic mother and an authoritarian father, she learned to be the good daughter who did what she was supposed to do. Getting married was one of those things. Another was never getting "unmarried."

So, at age twenty-five, Carol married exactly the right man. He fit the role, and to her at that time, fitting the role was more important than whether she loved him. "I'm not sure I ever really loved him," Carol said. "I was so shut down at that time in my life that maybe I couldn't have loved anybody."

Carol believes that her marriage lasted as long as it did because she put her husband on a pedestal. She idolized him. "I was first and foremost Mrs. Robert Swanson, totally identified with that role and with the ring on my finger." To go with the "perfect" marriage, Carol wanted to create the "perfect" family, so she had children and proceeded to become the "perfect" wife and mother. She was able to do all of this because, as she later discovered, she stayed out of her body, out of awareness. Completely focused on meeting the needs of her husband and children, Carol didn't know what she wanted as an individual. "Lack of personal awareness was the vital thing that allowed me to stay so long in that marriage."

In her late thirties, Carol had an experience that changed her life. She and her husband attended a marriage and family encounter weekend at their church. At this encounter, Carol learned about the concept of feelings, and, for the first time in her life, she began to experience self-awareness. She loved the experience, but unfortunately, her husband did not. So with Carol's growing self-awareness, tension grew in the marriage. Carol said, "Robert came down the pedestal a notch or two in my eyes, maybe more."

The Challenge of Role and Identity

As Carol continued to have ideas different from Robert, their relationship gradually deteriorated. Up until that time, she was still trying to be the good girl and do everything right. "I had basically just thought what he thought; now, for the first time, I had my own thoughts, as well as my own feelings." And that caused problems. Carol and Robert began to disagree, especially on parenting. He wanted to continue as the authoritarian parent, using physical punishment and demanding immediate obedience. She no longer agreed with that.

Until then, Carol said, they never fought. In fact, they never talked about much of anything. But when Carol changed, that changed. They started to have "discussions," but were never able to reach an understanding. He refused to change.

For a while, Carol handled this by sliding back into the old, familiar place of unawareness and just plodded on. But gradually, the marriage became more distant. Robert started working 70 to 80 hours a week and was rarely home. Finally, Carol couldn't take it anymore, and said to him, "We can do one of three things: We can continue as we are, and I don't want to do that. We can get a divorce, and I don't want to do that. Or we can go to counseling, and that's what I want to do." He responded,

"Well, then we will get a divorce." And they did. In Robert's mind, there was no backing off.

Carol reflected on this time: "So, here I was at age forty with three teenaged kids, and suddenly I had no marriage. Divorce wasn't in my script. I had lost my total identity. Taking off my ring was the most excruciating thing I ever did in my life. I went into an emotional free fall. It was devastating because if I was no longer the "perfect wife" with the "perfect family," who was I? I took total blame for the demise of the marriage, and for the next few years, I struggled with continual sorrow and shame."

On top of all that, Carol faced financial problems. Because she blamed herself for the divorce, she hadn't fought hard enough for decent child support. She had to get a job and was fortunate enough to get one in a role she could handle comfortably and well. The early years were really rough. The kids suffered. Carol knew it, but didn't have the energy to deal with it. It was all she could do to put food on the table.

Through all this, Carol continued to grow and to become more self-confident and self-aware. Slowly, she moved out of the role of wife, which had defined her for many years and began to see herself in other roles, ones more authentic, growing from the center of herself rather than focused on other people. Eventually she went back to school, got a master's degree, and opened her own business making her happier than she had ever been. Carol laughingly admitted, "It took me ten years to realize that by insisting on the divorce, Robert had given me the best gift I've ever gotten—myself!"

Mother

For those of us who have children, midlife brings us face to face with other challenges. Our children, to whom we have devoted so many years of our lives, grow up and begin their own lives. If their lives go well, they will quickly become absorbed with their own families and careers. Our roles change. We miss our old role as head of the family, but we are also relieved of the perpetual, grinding responsibilities of parenting young children. For many of us, it is a bittersweet moment. We relish our freedom, but the house seems lonely and empty. When it's finally "our turn," we're not sure what to do with it.

If our children's lives do not go well, if they are still at home or closely connected to home when it's time for them to be on their own, we face different challenges. We struggle with how much to help, when to let go, and on a deeper level, how to extract our own psyches from those of our children. We discover first hand that, even as the roles shift and our children no longer need us as "mother," the emotional bonds between us are forever, age notwithstanding. In our hearts, our children are always our children. When they hurt, we hurt. But now, it's even harder. When they were little, we could do something about their pain, but now, we're helpless. It's like having a piece of our own flesh out there in the world getting battered and bruised, and we can't do anything about it. Our children are adults, and only they can do what needs to be done to fix their lives. We can only love them and hope. . .and get out of their way.

And in the midst of all this, the inner drive for meaning, which for years may have been satisfied by mothering young children, returns at midlife with renewed force. For many years, we were pressured to stuff our own feelings and devote our lives to the care of others. Now we crave to live. But what can we do? We face a new challenge. If we're no longer needed as mothers, who are we? Can we reconnect with that young girl we once were, feel her energy, and regain her hopes and dreams about life? Can we pick up where we left off and move on with our own lives, even if our children are still struggling with theirs? Can we overcome our maternal guilt, find a balance between supporting others and living our own lives? Can we face down our fears, heed the call for inner growth, and create new lives for ourselves? Following is how one woman handled these challenges.

Marla's father and mother were both perfectionists and demanded that from their daughter. In Marla's family, it was always expected that everyone do the right thing in the right way. So, to get the security and love that she needed as a child, she became the "good girl." She learned this lesson well. Perfectionism became a central theme of her life, sometimes a strength, but at other times an obstacle to her health and happiness.

As the oldest child, Marla was always expected to take care of everybody—not only her three younger sisters, but also her mother, who, because of a difficult childhood, was insecure and emotionally needy. From the beginning, Marla's mother leaned on her for emotional support, leading Marla to feel that it was her job to take care of her mother. In many ways, she became her mother's mother.

The situation worsened when Marla's sister, Cora, was born. Marla described her as being almost uncontrollable from birth, a pathological liar, always defying everybody and taking huge, crazy risks like jumping on the back of a garbage truck when she was five years old. "My mother could never control her," Marla said, "so that became my job."

Tragically in her early teenage years, Cora was in an accident that left her permanently crippled and brain damaged. Through all of this, Marla learned to put her own needs aside and become the supportive person who took care of others. So, along with perfectionism, caretaking became a central theme of Marla's life.

Marla met Stan the summer she turned fifteen. Three years later they were married. "At the time," Marla remembers," I was drawn to him because he was rebellious, which I loved but didn't have the courage to do, and my father loved him, so that was a way to please my father. Later, I realized that the main reason I married Stan was because he needed me. He needed a mother, and I knew how to be a mother."

So Marla became Stan's "mother," and for a while that worked. The problems began when she became pregnant with their first child and became somebody else's mother. Marla believes that Stan never forgave her for that, and that he dealt with this by turning to his work, which kept him away much of the time and prevented him from ever really bonding with the children. Left with much of the responsibility of parenting and running the house on her own, Marla was torn between her career, her children, and her marriage, struggling to make everything right. "I wasn't happy," Marla remembers, "but divorce was inconceivable to me because I was the 'perfect' daughter and mother, and I just couldn't do that."

When the end finally came and her husband left, Marla was devastated. "I never thought he would leave," she said, and then, speaking softly, as if she had never fully realized it before, she added, "and I guess I couldn't leave."

In the years after the divorce, Marla felt the added pressure of being the only parent. She tried to be the perfect mother, but underneath, she was lonely and conflicted. "I was always trying to make up for Stan not being there. I was doing what was expected of me and more, because he wasn't doing his share. Secretly, I rebelled, but the practical part took care of me. I thought I had life all under control. I couldn't admit otherwise."

Now at age sixty-three with the kids all grown up, Marla finds herself still struggling with the same conflicts. She craves freedom but can't quite let go of the role of mother as the kids still lean on her too much. "When my phone rings at night, my stomach gets tight because I'm thinking, 'who is it and what do they want from me?' It's like part of me wants to run away, find that little cabin in the mountains where I can just be me, but part of me is afraid of not being needed because then what? Who am I? I have based my whole life on somebody needing me. That gave me a sense of importance and place and security. It's a familiar role. That's how I identified myself."

Marla's conflict was made worse by the guilt she felt for not providing her children with a "perfect" family. She finds herself still trying to make things right by being there for her children and grandchildren all the time, and by telling them over and over how sorry she is for the man she picked for their father.

Yet Marla realizes that because of the divorce, she has grown in ways that she otherwise might not have. Even as divorce forced her to live on her own, it set her free to be her real self. Over the years, Marla worked hard on her personal growth and developed supportive relationships with other women who were also on the path of personal growth. "All my life I had to sit on my 'spark' but now I'm more aware of what I really want and freer from my compulsions. I have more options. I'm also more understanding and accepting of myself and others, and more content with life. I find myself turning more toward my work and feeling a pull to go within for my spirituality. For the first time in my life, I'm confident and have a sense of pride in myself. I am what I am, and that's enough."

Whether we have embodied the identity of Mother, Spouse, Caretaker, Breadwinner, Career Woman, Peacemaker, or some other, in our own way, we lose ourselves in the roles we played in the Second Act. At midlife, we are faced with a wake-up call and a challenge: Will you acknowledge that the roles you have lived for many years are over? And what will you do about it?

You can choose to look backward, hanging onto old roles while denying the reality of the changes that have occurred in your life. Or you can push past denial, see your life in the present, and with that vision, create a new role for yourself, one that expresses *who you are now*, while drawing deeply from the wisdom gained over the years.

 ## Reflect

What roles have you lived that have ended?

Have you released them? If not, can you move through denial into a new identity, one that is present-oriented and brings you happiness?

Who are you now? How do you define your current roles?

10

The Challenge of the Body

For many women, the stark change in roles and identity demanded of us at midlife is the hardest challenge. But lives differ, and for me, the hardest challenges came in my body during the inevitable physical decline of later life.

When we move into midlife, we all face profound changes in our body. Perhaps it's safe to say that all of the changes are unwelcomed because they all say "you're getting old," a message we don't want to hear. Physical decline is an inevitable part of aging. On the surface, it seems purely negative—painful, scary, debilitating, and disruptive of our "normal" lives. But if you take the trouble to look underneath all this, you may find, as I did, that physical decline also offers an opportunity to rebuild the connection to our bodies that, for most women, was lost in the hustle and bustle of life in the Second Act.

During the first part of our lives, most of us live comfortably in our bodies, unconsciously relying on it to do whatever we want it to do, never dreaming that our bodies would do anything less. We took our bodies for granted.

Next in midlife, we discover that our bodies are not as cooperative as they used to be. Along with various aches and pains, our joints lack the easy mobility of years past, especially when we wake up in the morning and take that first long, stiff walk to the bathroom wondering what happened to the body that used to leap eagerly out of bed every morning without a twinge.

We no longer have our old and seemingly limitless energy and vitality. We find that the way we heedlessly packed our days with one activity after another simply doesn't work anymore. We get tired, and we're forced to consider just how much we can do. If we don't consider it, if we continue to force ourselves beyond our capacity, we find our bodies making the decision for us, sometimes with chronic fatigue so severe that it becomes difficult to do anything at all.

In addition, many of us face serious illness or injury. When we were young, we felt invulnerable. Now we know this isn't so. By midlife, our lifestyles catch up with us, forcing us to deal with health issues that are often terrifying, painful, and limiting.

We are challenged to slow down and listen to our bodies. Aside from the boost this gives to our health, this allows us to enjoy the small things of life, to "smell the roses," and to actually have time to reflect on our lives, think our own thoughts, and feel our own feelings, perhaps for the first time in years. In reconnecting with our bodies, we discover a new strength, one that is not dependent on what happens around us but in our own inner self. The challenge of physical decline becomes a gift.

Two physical challenges, both in my fifties, ushered in the rediscovery of my body. I say "rediscovery" because as a child I was strongly connected to my body. I identified with it in the sense that I thought of my body as "me." It was my body that rode bikes, roller-skated, played ball, jumped rope and climbed my beloved sycamore tree.

Then, after a few years in my Second Act, the pressures of the outside world forced me to disconnect from myself. As I discussed in Chapter 7, by the time I reached my early thirties, I had become so unaware of my body that I sailed through a serious "little stroke," unconscious of the potential message it held for me. So when I reached midlife, I was overdue for some wake-up calls. They came in the form most likely to gain my attention: challenges to my physical health.

My first challenge, appropriately enough, came in my heart. I remember clearly the moment it started. I was cleaning the house, and in my typically perfectionist way, I was leaning over to dust some obscure corner that only I would notice when my heart signaled for my attention with a jolting "whomp." It got my attention alright, even though I tried to ignore it.

Well, my heart wouldn't be ignored. It kept on whomping, and even added some episodes of racing. Now I couldn't ignore it, and much to my dismay, I also couldn't control it. For the first time in my life I had the feeling that was to become a familiar experience in the next several years: I felt like I was trapped in a body that was foreign to me, disconnected from what I thought of as "myself," and therefore, totally out of my control. What was this body going to put me through? I had no idea, but whatever it was, I feared I didn't have what it would take to get through it. I felt completely alone.

And so began my "heart journey," which led me through several doctors' visits, a scary trip to the ER, and a short stay in the hospital for tests. I particularly

The Challenge of the Body

remember one night in the hospital, lying by myself on what had to be the world's most uncomfortable bed with my heart monitored to the nursing station, imagining all the awful possibilities that may await me while the night nurses chatted and laughed among themselves. At that moment I no longer felt a part of their carefree world, the world of youth that I once lived in. I had entered that dark, scary world of aging. I knew aging happened to other people, but I never imagined it would actually happen to me.

Up to that point in life, the tools I had been given to cope with life had worked fairly well, and when they didn't, I had learned to cover up or compensate. But for what I was now facing, there was no cover-up. People could give me support, but no one else could go through this for me. I was terrified.

Friends and family tried to help. I remember that my husband brought me a book, something about healing the heart. It was sweet of him, and I acted appreciative, but the truth was that I was too scared to bring myself to read it. A friend brought me a tape of beautiful piano music that I listened to all the next day as I lay on my bed looking out the window at some treetops that seemed especially beautiful. And for the time being, I was comforted, not realizing I was experiencing one of those soft, peaceful moments that would become one of the joys and an important source of strength in my New Third Act.

Finally, after all the tests were over and all the specialists had their say, it turned out that my diagnosis was not life threatening and could be controlled through regular small doses of a beta blocker, which I take to this day. It took a long time, but eventually my panic subsided. Now, my heart is fairly quiet, but when it does act up, I experience it as an old friend whose whomps, twitters, and bumps no longer scare me. Sometimes I even remember to listen to them and open myself to the message they bring from my heart to my "disconnected" body—"rest, relax, and stay present."

For a while, I was comfortable, so much so that I almost forgot the lessons that I had learned on my "heart journey." I was due for another wake-up call, and indeed, one came in my early '50s, but this time was a little longer and scarier than the first.

It began in my legs. One day while driving home from my office, I noticed my legs felt weak, especially when I held down the clutch and brake while stopping at traffic lights. I began to worry a bit but tried to put it out of my mind. That didn't work because gradually I began to notice not only weakness but also numbness and occasional tingling in my legs.

The Challenge of the Body

Then things got worse. The symptoms spread to my arms, up my neck, and into my jaw and the back of my head. My jaw began to feel numb to the point that my speech was a little affected. About a week later, I remember talking with a friend about it, hoping for an encouraging reply like, "Oh, I've felt that; it's nothing," or "You're probably overreacting to something that's minor." But instead, she said, "Wow! That would scare me!" Then I really was scared, and although I hoped it would all just go away, needless to say, it didn't. In fact, it got worse.

In addition to numbness and tingling, I began having nighttime seizure-like episodes—my body trembled, my teeth clinched, and the muscles in my arms and legs pulled into tight knots. The worst part was that these episodes occurred late at night while others were sleeping, and I had to go through them all alone. I didn't want to wake up my husband or young son for fear they would worry, and no one would get any sleep. Lying on the couch in the living room curled up and shaking, I imagined all the horrible diseases I could have.

One night in particular, I was lying on the couch shaking when I suddenly thought, "I want my mother!" But that wasn't possible; my mother was dead. Remembering her only made the fear worse because she wasn't there and would never be there again. And for a moment, I felt that strange sense of disorientation and unreality I had experienced after her death as if I was floating in a void, arms and legs flailing, reaching for something solid, something that wasn't there. The world felt false and strange with no guide posts and nothing to cling to.

Then I remembered that even if my mother had been there, she couldn't have given me the support I needed at this time. She was good in many ways. If she were here, she would do things for me and worry with me, but when it came to emotional support, she wasn't so great. But I still wanted a mother. I wanted what I imagined a mother to be—warm, comforting, reassuring—a mother that would somehow make it all okay. Isn't that what a mother does?

But then, like me, I realized everybody wants a mother, an ideal mother, but nobody actually has one. And for some reason that thought was a little comforting. I'm not alone; I'm feeling what everybody feels.

Still, the fact remained that whatever was going to happen to me I had to face alone. Others could support, but nobody could do it for me. That, essentially, is the challenge of midlife. Unlike in the Second Act where, difficult as life could be at times, we still had our dreams, hopes, and fantasies to gloss over life's realities, in the New Third Act, we must face life straight on.

So, the next morning I called the orthopedist. I remember the first appointment. I described what I felt in my arms and legs while he kept examining my back.

"No," I said. "It's my legs."

"It's your back," he said. In spite of my protests, he calmly maintained, "No, it's your back."

Of course, he was right. After the x-ray, he told me the problem—I was getting older. The vertebrae in my back were disintegrating and compressing my spinal nerves, causing the symptoms I experienced. He mentioned surgery, which terrified me, but then said that I could probably fix it with exercise. He recommended daily walking, building up to five miles twice a day. He also gave me some strengthening and stretching exercises, and for a while I had to wear a neck brace and back support.

I guess most people would have been discouraged by the thought of walking five miles twice a day, but to tell the truth, I was so traumatized by this experience that all I felt was relief. There was hope! The doctor was telling me that I didn't have some horrible disease, and that I could heal myself by walking. I was willing to try anything, so I did what he said. We were in the middle of a hot and humid Georgia summer, but I got up early every morning and walked, and then in the evening when it was cooler, I walked again, gradually building up to five miles twice a day. It took a while, but over time, the symptoms diminished, I gave up my braces and supports, and my fear abated.

That was twenty years ago, and still to this day, I'm a daily walker. I no longer do five miles twice a day, but walking and evening exercises are a regular part of my life. Several years later, a follow-up x-ray showed my spine to be in very good shape, and the doctor commented to me, "You'll never know how much good you've done yourself with these daily walks, not only for your back, but also your heart."

And so what started as horrible experiences turned into positive ones. As a result of both of these health challenges that I faced early in my midlife, I gained valuable experience. I woke up from my denial, accepted the challenges, and made the choices that would lead me back to health. Once again I live in my body as I had in my childhood, but with an important difference—I no longer take my body for granted. And in the process, I developed inner strength that I did not have before that time.

I am sure that all of us have had issues with our bodies as we move through midlife. Gradually, we come to realize that physical issues in some form will be a part of the rest of our lives, and we must be aware of our bodies and care for them on a daily basis. We know that someday the diagnosis will not be so benign.

So every day, when I wake up in the morning, step on the floor, and feel my legs holding the weight of my body as my heart beats in my chest, I send a prayer of gratitude for the wonderful body that has taken me so far in life.

Reflect:

What were your body's wake-up calls? How did you answer them? What, if anything, did you learn?

How did these physical events change how you approach aging? Did this make you more anxious or calm?

What new awareness—physical, mental, or emotional—has come to you during the "slowing down" process?

11

The Challenge of Loss

When we're young and busy creating our lives, we're focused on fun and excitement of what the future will bring. We don't want to deal with anything that's a "downer." And so, most of us deny or minimize our losses and put them behind us as quickly as we can. Or so we think.

Later as adults, we're busy with families and careers, taking care of others' needs, finding ways to get ahead, or struggling just to get by. When we do encounter rough times, our focus is on getting through them, fixing them, and putting them behind us so we can deal with the next crisis. We don't have time to grieve. Indeed, most of us don't understand the process of grief or the valuable purpose it serves in helping us let go of the past and clear our psyches for new growth. We don't realize that ungrieved losses don't go away. They simply lie buried within us where they sap our energy and exert a chronic negative drag on our lives.

As a result, when we reach midlife, we suffer from emotional pile-up, the accumulation of a lifetime of unhealed losses. In my mind's eye, I imagine these losses packed into a tight little box somewhere deep in our psyches, all squeezed together and entangled with each other underneath a bulging lid. By midlife that box is crammed full and requires more and more energy to hold down the lid at a time when our body is in decline and less able to supply that energy.

What are we to do? We can't stuff more unhealed losses because there's no more room in the box. We can't avoid them because they are inevitable and universal. And we can't ignore them because they are terrifying. At this point we have a choice: we can either allow ourselves to be dragged down into an endless decline of depression and despair, or we can face our losses, grieve them, and let them go. Then we can open ourselves to the new possibilities ahead.

So, what are these losses that are inevitable, universal, and often terrifying?

Loss of Loved Ones

When we reflect on losses, our first thoughts are often of losing loved ones: parents, spouses, siblings, relatives, friends, and sometimes even children. Many of us would include beloved pets in that category. These losses can be shocking and deeply painful. This is particularly true of losses which defy the "regular" order of things, like the death of a child while parents who generally would have preceded the child in death are left to suffer the loss for the rest of their lives. Other losses, such as the death of grandparents, seem more natural and may be easier to absorb. In any case, the loss of a loved one always impacts our lives, sometimes profoundly and permanently.

One difficult midlife loss that many of us face is the loss of our parents. There are many ways besides death to lose one's parents, like illness and injury, for example. Parents who suffer with a disability, a common experience in old age, are no longer able to fill their longtime role as supporters or caretakers in times of need or their symbolic role of head of the family, protecting the old traditions. Christmas dinner or Seder feasts can no longer be held at Granny's house. But, conversely, a feeble parent can no longer be the formidable critic who could always stop us in our tracks. And so we are forced to face many conflicting feelings—shock, sadness, anger, relief—and the inevitable guilt that accompanies them.

One of the most difficult ways to lose a parent is through dementia. I lost my father this way, so I know the pain of being with a parent who is present, but "not there."

My parents had lived in Ohio for their entire lives, but after my father's retirement, they moved to St. Petersburg, Florida. My father loved Florida, but unfortunately he had only a few years to enjoy this new life before he began his five-year decline into dementia. He remained physically strong until the very end, but after two years into the disease, he no longer remembered who I was, much less that he even had a daughter. When I took my infant son to visit him, my father cried, but whether in joy or sadness I never knew because he was no longer able to speak. These years were unspeakably difficult for all of us, but especially for my mother who kept my father at home with her for the full five years. Finally, after suffering a massive stroke, he passed away peacefully on September 16, 1972. Though his death was a relief to us all, it was also deeply sad. He was the kindest man I have ever known, and he deserved better. And now he is gone, and I never got a chance for him to hear and understand me say "Goodbye, Daddy. I really, really love you."

On October 5, 1987, fifteen years after my father died, my mother died of a stroke at age eighty. Unlike my father's long, slow demise, my mother's death came quickly, yet with a sad, ironic twist. For years, my mother had longed to return to Ohio to be near a beloved sister, surrounded by the community and neighborhood that had been her home for over thirty years. But she was conflicted. Moving to Ohio meant leaving Elsie, her other sister, who was living with her at the time and wanted to stay in Florida. Finally, they agreed that Elsie would move into a senior living center in St. Petersburg and my mother would move back to Ohio.

But it was not to be. Two days before she was to leave, Mother dropped a piece of toast while eating breakfast, reached down to pick it up, toppled onto the floor, and broke her hip. And that quirky little accident was the beginning of the end. She had surgery, followed by a debilitating blood chemical imbalance, and finally a severe stroke. Two weeks later she was dead. Of course I will never know, but I really believe, that my mother's "quirky little accident" and subsequent death was her way of resolving an inner conflict that, in life, she could never really resolve—she wanted to move but didn't want to abandon Elsie, so she resolved it by leaving the scene.

My mother's death was much more difficult for me than my father's death had been. Although I was with her for most of that last two weeks, she was sick and delirious most of the time, leaving us little opportunity to talk. Then, one evening when I had slipped out for a bite to eat, she passed away. And once again, I had lost a parent without a chance to say goodbye or tell her how much I loved her.

What does it feel like to lose your parents? It's amazing, but no matter how old you may be or how disconnected you have become from your parents' lives, losing them is a shock that reverberates deep within one's gut. The loss leaves you with a deep emptiness like no other. If you haven't yet experienced it, you can hardly fathom how it will feel to not have a mother or a father, to essentially be an orphan in this world, to know that "home" is gone forever with a completeness that you have never before felt.

Just as no one can tell us ahead of time how it will feel to give birth to another human being, I can hardly find the words to describe what it's like to be parentless. For me, it was strange and scary in a whole new way, knowing that I couldn't pick up the phone and call Mother ever again.

For me, one of the most unnerving parts of the experience came when I suddenly realized that *I* was now part of the oldest generation. Many family members looked up to me as the family matriarch, the spot that my parents used to fill. I definitely didn't feel ready for that role. I also began to notice that when I walked into a room, I was often the oldest one there, and that many of my friends looked up to me as a wisdom figure capable of helping them solve their life problems. I felt the ground shift from under me as I worked to accommodate myself to this new position in life.

I believe that the loss of our parents is one of the defining moments of the New Third Act. How we respond to this loss—whether we avoid our feelings and shut down, or face it squarely and open to a new level of experience—helps determine the direction and quality of our lives in midlife and beyond.

Loss of Youth and Beauty

There are other inevitable losses in the New Third Act that confront us with many painful experiences and permanently change our lives. One of these is the loss of our youthful beauty and strength.

Remember the moment when you looked in the mirror and saw that first gray hair? Or you noticed the first wrinkles around your eyes or mouth? You can't help but see that you are no longer the young woman whose reflection you admired twenty, thirty, or forty years ago. For many, the worst shock comes when you realize that you're beginning to look like your mother!

My first experience with this realization came at my thirtieth high school reunion. When I walked into the room expecting to see classmates that I hadn't seen in thirty years, I was shocked to see not them, but their parents! On second glance, I saw that these were indeed the friends of my youth who now looked like their parents. And then it dawned on me that they might be thinking the same of me. Until that moment, I hadn't fully grasped that I was no longer the high school kid that I see in my mind's eye; I was a middle-aged woman, at least on the outside. On the inside, I simply felt like my usual self. I suppose my reunion friends felt the same way. To add to the irony, while I was busy talking to old friends, my husband was busy calculating weight. It turned out that our reunion group of about forty people had collectively gained four hundred and sixty pounds over the last thirty years.

Yes, weight is another issue. Over the years, most of us manage to "put on a few," as the saying goes. During the super-active years of our Second Act when we were busy managing everybody else's health and wellbeing, we somehow managed to neglect our own. And now when we may have more time to care for ourselves, we discover that, unlike when we were in our twenties, taking off those extra pounds isn't so easy. But it's not just the weight, it's where that weight is situated. The small waist and flat abs of our younger years have been replaced by spare tires and a little—or not so little— tummy. Somehow our youth has slipped away, and we're faced with the painful realization that our bodies have taken on a new shape.

Coming to terms with all this is not easy, and it's made even harder by the realization that the change is permanent. Of course we can—and hopefully most of us do—work to keep our bodies in shape with our goals now focused on maintaining health rather than regaining youthful beauty. Caring for our bodies, especially exercising on a regular basis and maintaining a healthy diet, takes time and effort. Our schedules must change.

Physical care must be our first concern, the top item on our daily "to do" list. Other activities, perhaps ones that we would prefer to engage in, must move down the list to make room for new priorities.

On the surface, losing one's youth and beauty may seem trivial compared to the loss of loved ones. But the fact is that our culture places a lot of value on the image of women's beauty. In many of the myths and fairy tales to which we are exposed, this image is contrasted to that of the ugly old woman who is sometimes depicted as an evil witch. The moral is simple and clear—"young" is beautiful and good while "old" is ugly and bad. Though this is more important to some women than to others, all of us are affected by it. From the time we were young girls, "the look"—the current cultural image of the beautiful young woman—is slammed in our face everywhere we turn.

Is it surprising that so many women dread being "old?" The modern cosmetics industry makes a fortune on this fear, providing women with thousands of ways to maintain a soft, wrinkle-free complexion, transform gray hair into numerous shades of blonde or brunette, and, with the help of plastic surgery, restore the youthful face and figure that once was ours. The truth is, however, that we aren't young anymore, and try as we might, there's no way we can be. We can't turn back the clock; we're getting older. In the words of a feisty old woman I once knew, "Well, ya cain't hep it, honey. Ya jest keep on goin' up."

Does that mean you should throw away your cosmetics and never try to enhance your appearance? No. It simply means the choice is up to you. You should feel free to use or not to use cosmetics, clothes, hair dyes, and all that's available to enhance your appearance as who you *are,* not who you *were.* As women in midlife or beyond, we have a beauty all our own, a beauty based less on superficial characteristics, and more on the depth of soul that shines through our eyes and the wisdom revealed by the fine lines of our faces. Above all, let your beauty reflect your unique personality. Embrace the glorious freedom that comes with getting older when we no longer govern our lives by what others think, but rather by what we feel and know in our own inner selves.

Loss of Hopes and Dreams

For all of us, one of the most difficult challenges we face at this time of life is the loss of our hopes and dreams from earlier years. Sometime during the course of our midlife, we may find ourselves asking, "What happened to my dream of an exciting career or a perfect family? When did it get lost? How did I get to where I am now? Is this all there is?" Often our lives are not as fulfilling as we had hoped or expected, leaving us disappointed and wondering, "Where did I go wrong?"

If our lives have dealt us really savage blows like illness, death, and failures, we may blame our unhappiness on that, thinking if all had gone according to plan, we would be satisfied and happy. But even if we have had the life that we thought we wanted, we often still feel empty. All looks well on the outside, but on the inside, we feel a deep sense of loss for which we often blame ourselves—"I have everything that I always wanted, and I'm still not happy. What's wrong with me?"

Could it be that the hopes and dreams of our youth turned out not to be what we really wanted? Perhaps they were passed on to us by our elders and/or the circumstances of our lives, and we, unknowingly, adopted them as our own. We learned the proper moves to make it in the game of life, so we succeeded in creating the "perfect life." Somehow it still wasn't satisfying. It didn't come from our core self, and therefore didn't express who we truly are. At midlife, the emptiness that had always lingered deep inside us forces its way to the surface and demands to be recognized.

Or could it be that we have driven ourselves so relentlessly to create the perfect life that we've never taken time to really enjoy it? Then, suddenly at midlife, we realize that something's wrong with *that* picture. We're not having any fun yet! And so, we may decide that it's time to slow down, look around, and begin to live, not just exist. And when we do that, we may realize that our "perfect life" isn't so perfect after all. We may find ourselves setting out in a whole new direction based on a whole new set of hopes and dreams. Or at the very least, we may find that our "perfect life" could use a few little nips and tucks that express our newly updated version.

Perhaps some of us were fortunate enough to actually live the life of our dreams only to find those dreams have lost their luster at midlife. We feel restless and discontented. Something is missing, but what? We don't know how to proceed. We are in a classic midlife quandary—our original hopes and dreams no longer satisfy. We've grown beyond them to something new.

No matter how we have lived our lives to this point, at midlife something must change. In fact, whether we will it or not, something *does* change inside of us, and it's up to us to recognize that change and to build new lives around it. We must be willing to re-examine the hopes and dreams of our youth, and if necessary, to let them go, grieve the loss, and open ourselves to the new possibilities that the New Third Act offers.

Loss of an Unlimited Future

When we were in the First Act, we lived our lives facing forward into a vast unknown but exciting future with plenty of time to build dreams, drop them if they didn't work, and build others to suit our wants and needs. Life felt infinite.

In the Second Act, the future is clouded over with the demands of everyday life, but we still thought of life as moving forward, perhaps toward goals we set for ourselves, such as job promotions and college for our children. Almost unnoticed, the years gradually pass by.

Then one day we wake up to find ourselves in midlife, perhaps in our fifties or sixties, and we realize with a jolt that our lives are half over or maybe more than half. With each passing day our options for the future narrow, and we regret the lost opportunities of the past. Building new hopes and dreams becomes even more urgent when we realize that our future is no longer unlimited.

This is a tough time for women. Nobody wants to think about getting old, because, well, nobody likes "old women." In fact, nobody cares much for middle-aged

The Challenge of Loss

women either because, after years of being nice and looking pretty and not going after what we wanted, we've had it. We do as we please and don't much care anymore what others think We'd like to get going with living *our* lives, but just when we're ready to take on the world, we suddenly realize that time is running out.

That realization can be a good thing or a bad thing. It's a bad thing if we allow ourselves to be discouraged and hesitate to set new goals for our lives. In this passive state, we may sink into a depression that slowly absorbs our strength and eventually our lives. Or, we may allow ourselves to more or less ignore our current lives, shift our vision to the past, and dwell on the "good old days" while the real days, the ones that we're living now, slide by.

But it's a good thing if we use this realization to recognize what has always been true—that the present moment is all that we have. Yes, we can set our new goals, but once set, we don't dwell on them; we act on them. And, yes, we can enjoy sharing memories with family and old friends, but we don't let ourselves get stuck in the past. We live in the present, and we learn to treasure each moment as precious and irreplaceable. We embrace whatever comes our way, good or bad, as life—*our* life—to be lived to the fullest no matter what.

And so it is with all our losses. They bring us pain and grief, but also offer us opportunities. If we face our losses openly and honestly, grieve them, let them go, and open ourselves to what lies ahead, we will be enriched by the experience. Not only will we gain inner strength, but we will also awaken to a broader, fuller view of life, one that offers depth and complexity, perhaps even wisdom. In this way, the challenge of loss can become our greatest gift.

Reflect:

What did you discover as you examined, made an inventory of, and released your emotional pile-up of losses? Do you feel the freedom after this purge, and how are you utilizing the new energy?

How have you established "home" for yourself after losing your parents and/or others significant in your life?

How can you make peace, embrace, and even flaunt your new physical "look"?

How have you re-established your hopes and dreams in your New Third Act?

What are your new goals, and how are you living these in the present moment?

12

The Challenge of Authenticity

When we reach midlife, we may become aware of a pressure rising within us, pushing up from deep inside. We find ourselves longing for something we cannot name, something that will bring meaning into our lives, make us feel alive in ways we have not for many years, perhaps since our childhood—perhaps never. That pressure is our inner self, our true self, our soul crying out to live before it is too late, before time runs out. We face the challenge of authenticity.

For those of us who by virtue of good fortune and personal effort no longer need to struggle to survive and have grown past the stage of needing the approval of others, the pressure to become authentic is universal. We may not choose to heed the pressure; we may not even allow ourselves to be conscious of it. Nevertheless, it is there, pushing to get our attention.

The pressure comes to us in many ways. We may feel it in our daily lives when it becomes increasingly difficult for us to put on the old social masks and walk through the roles that once had meaning but have become stale and tedious. We may find ourselves resisting the daily tasks that everyone expects of us, tasks we once performed without a second thought. Women who had always loved preparing delicious, healthful meals for their families may suddenly find that not only do they hate to cook, but they also can't stand to go near a grocery store. As one woman put it, "My refrigerator is almost empty, and I really don't care. If I'm hungry, I eat out or pick up a frozen dinner that I eat at home while I watch TV." Can we do what this woman did? Can we let go of our old habits and allow ourselves to be led by the new voices opening within us?

We may find ourselves annoyed and bored with long-time friendships, noticing, as if for the first time, how shallow and unfulfilling these relationships really are. "What did we ever see in these people?" we ask ourselves. We struggle with the conflict between loyalty to old friends and our need for something deeper and more

The Challenge of Authenticity

meaningful. Which shall we do: take the easy path of salving the feelings of others while ignoring what we really want, or make the difficult choice to be true to ourselves even though it may hurt others' feelings?

We may long for something new in our lives. The career that once excited and challenged us has lost its luster, and the goals that we worked so hard to achieve no longer seem so important to us. We may long to express ourselves creatively but don't know where to begin. Perhaps, over the years of ignoring our own feelings, we may have come to believe that we have nothing creative within us. Yet something inside us cries out for a new adventure, but we don't know what that is. Or if we do know, we pull back out of fear. We are reluctant to leave the comfort zone we've worked so long to create, even though that comfort zone has now become a prison, holding us close to the safe and familiar, preventing us from moving forward to engage with life on our own terms. Do we have the courage to do this?

Often we may find our thoughts floating back to our childhood, remembering the easy sense of self we had before we moved into the demanding roles and responsibilities of adulthood. What happened to the little girls we once were? We've changed—or have we? Can we reclaim some of that childhood energy that led us naturally to feel what we felt, to know what we wanted, to be who we really were?

If we are to lead a fulfilling life in the New Third Act, the answer to all these questions must be "yes." But it won't be easy. To be authentic, we must be conscious, being aware of all that's inside of us, good and bad. Of course, all of us would rather not be aware of our painful memories, but if we aren't aware of them, we won't be able to heal them. Unless we've consciously remembered and released the painful feelings around each memory, it's just buried and using up lots of our energy to keep it there.

We would also rather not be aware of our dark side, even though we all have one. It's just part of being human. The dark side, by the way, is that part of us that's not very nice, that part that sees all the faults of others but manages not to notice the not-so-nice things that we do. Our dark side is there whether we admit or not, causing untold problems in our lives, especially in our relationships with others. But to be authentic, to be true to ourselves and to others, we must open our eyes to everything and own all that we are, both good and bad. That's authenticity.

The Challenge of Authenticity

I believe there is something inside all of us that is hungry to live authentically. We ache to satisfy this hunger but realize that it will require difficult work on our part. It may even require us to change our lives in ways that we aren't sure we're ready to face. We must either do the work that leads to meaningful, authentic lives, or avoid the work and sink into resignation and decline. My hope is that each of us will choose to live authentically—no matter what.

We have arrived at The Choice.

Reflect:

How have you experienced the pressure to utilize this golden chance to become authentic?

What signs have you noticed of your life changing to a life more authentic? Loss of old friendships and gaining of new ones? Desires for new learning and opportunities? Flashbacks to the joy of childhood? Yearnings to be more creative?

What goals are you contemplating for your New Third Act?

13

The Third Act Choice

As we come to the end of midlife and begin to move into our Third Act, we are faced with these questions: Who am I now? How will I live my remaining years?

We have arrived at The Choice, a crossroads in our life that offers us two paths: the Path of Resignation or the Path of Growth. We are free to choose either one.

If we choose the Path of Resignation, we will live our Third Act years in the old traditional roles. For most women that means staying safe and secure in a life that we understand and does not challenge us, one that follows the path expected of us at "our age." We avoid risks like traveling to places we've always wanted to see, meeting new friends, going back to school, starting a new career, or embarking on anything we've always wanted

The Third Act Choice

Traditional Third Act	New Third Act
Path of Resignation	*Path of Growth*
Remain in Old Traditional Roles	*Create a New Authentic Life*
Offers Illusions of Safety	*Requires Courage & Commitment*
DECLINE	***GROWTH***

to do but never had the time or the nerve. The conventional way is easier, but comes at a cost in happiness, fulfillment, and, possibly, health.

If we choose the Path of Growth, we will live authentically in the New Third Act, a way that offers the possibility of personal fulfillment, excitement, and meaning. We may choose to complete our education that was disrupted years ago by our Second Act responsibilities and start the career we always wanted—artist, writer, musician, business woman, politician, activist, or something that interests us and pulls us in an entirely new direction. We may find ourselves open to all the risks that a conventional life does not allow. The path of growth may be difficult and challenging. It requires courage and commitment. As you will see in the next section, you can learn how to strengthen yourself from the inside out, so you can take on the fulfilling life every women should experience.

> **The New Third Act can and will
> be the best time of all.**

Part Four
The New Third Act

14

The Path of Growth

If you have chosen the Path of Growth, I welcome you to the New Third Act!

When we were in the Second Act, busy with families and careers, the focus was on others and the external world. In the New Third Act, the focus is on us. We must learn to turn our attention inward, come to know our true selves and build the inner strength we need to express our truth in the world. We must resist the urge to hold on to what is past and build new pillars to support our present lives. We must be willing to live with uncertainty and ambiguity, and accept the fact that we have little control over our lives. We learn to control what we can and don't worry about the rest.

The New Third Act

The overriding goal in the New Third Act is to grow, to see life as it really is, to drop our preconceived ideas and projections, and live according to our own truths. The process of our growth is non-linear, flowing in a spiral, constantly moving forward and circling back on itself as it moves into deeper and broader realms. It is a journey, not a goal, because we never really get there, but are constantly expanding our horizons into our authentic self.

Moving into the New Third Act, although it is well worth it, can be a difficult transition, involving mental and emotional upheavals that can be frightening, confusing, and sometimes painful. When faced with these feelings, it is always a temptation to avoid or repress them. But in so doing, we only postpone the inevitable emotional adjustments that we must come to terms with while tying up the vital energy we need to help us cope in the present moment.

However, all is not negative. Transitions are also the most powerful moments of our lives because, during these times, we are open. This means we can change. Old mental structures break down making room for new growth and for moving our life in new directions. If we are conscious during these times, aware of our thoughts and feelings, we can steer our life in positive ways that further our growth and open us to exciting new possibilities.

In every life shift, we experience losses and gains. To fully grasp the meaning of the change, we must process both. We must recognize and grieve our losses, then acknowledge and celebrate what we have gained or hope to gain. That way we have a sense of where we've been and where we're going.

But as we move into the New Third Act, the most important thing of all is we must learn to live from the "inside out." This means we shift our focus from the external world to our inner experience and live from our real selves.

This transition is not easy, but at the same time, it the most natural thing in the world. Developmentally, we are ready to do this. Somewhere around fifty, the switch clicks on, and we know that we must do something different with our lives. We may not know what or how, but we feel the call.

We must develop the strength and wisdom to answer the call.

15

Healing and Transforming

I think of each woman's life as her own personal universe. Like the vast universe we all live in, our personal universe has a beginning, a birth—our personal "Big Bang"—and, like the universe we live in, we continue to grow as the years go by. When we are children, our universe is very small, time moves slowly, and for the most part, we see things only from our child's point of view. As we get older, our universe expands, time moves at an ever-increasing speed, life is more complex, and we see things from many perspectives. Everything that we've ever experienced is stored inside us; some of it is consciously available to us, some of it not, but nothing disappears.

It's strange but wonderful that, from our perspective as women in the New Third Act, we can access our inner self and experience our universe from any stage of our life. You can see a childhood event, feel it as a child, but more importantly, you can now understand it in a new and different way. Although the information is still there, it no longer has a hold on us. We can let it go.

Our first step to fulfillment in the New Third Act is to let go of the past so we can live fully in the present. Of course, this doesn't mean erasing things that happened in the past. Obviously, this can't be done. But what can be done is to change the way we see past events and how we allow them to affect our present lives. This often involves grieving to release feelings of loss, anger, sadness, even revenge or retribution as a way to reclaim our energy and experience our full vitality.

Another part of this step to bring us into the present is recognizing how we define and see ourselves as who we are in this moment.

Self-Image

We often resist shifting our self-image to reflect our current age. Although we are in midlife or beyond, we may continue to see ourselves as we were in our youth, in strong, healthy bodies that move with grace and ease, only to discover that our knees, hips, or back in our present bodies won't allow us to do that. Or, we may see ourselves as mothers, but now our children have grown and don't need a mother anymore. Or, we may feel comfortable and secure in our marriage, seeing ourselves as a contented wife, only to have a spouse die prematurely or to find ourselves faced with divorce. Or, we may have retired or been downsized from a job that had shaped our identity for years, leaving us dangling without a safety net, wondering who we are and what comes next.

The realization that we cannot do what we imagine ourselves doing or what we have always done in the past jolts our sense of reality. Who are we without our strong bodies, without our family, without our spouse, without our careers? Can we accept ourselves as we are at the moment and allow ourselves to move forward as the person that we are now?

When our present lives no longer match the self-image we carry around in our heads, we are confused and discouraged, and often compound the situation by blaming ourselves for not being the person we think we *should* be. We suffer internally, and our lives suffer as well, because if we cannot accept who we are now, we cannot be fully present in our current lives.

The New Third Act

Finding fulfillment in the New Third Act requires that we value ourselves as we are now, not as we once were, nor as we thought we should be in some perfect, unrealistic world. We must put aside past images and build new ones that are more in tune with our present selves. We must move past cultural stereotypes and allow ourselves to experience the beauty of older bodies and celebrate the glorious expansion of the soul that comes only with age. Each time we identify and flesh out a true image of our self—one that we respect and love—we become more empowered to live the life we want and to mentor other women who have also lost their way.

As I've grown older, I have experienced many struggles with my shifting self-image. One occurred during a late afternoon ten years ago as I was driving home from the office. I found my thoughts focusing, as they often had done over the past few years, on trying to make some sense of who I was. A month ago I had celebrated my seventieth birthday, and even though I didn't feel much different than I ever felt, I knew that I *was* different. The date on my birth certificate, as well as the aches and pains in my body, all made it clear that I was no longer young, but I just couldn't see myself as "old." Who was I?

As I pondered this, my mind floated back to a recent trip I had co-led with my friend, Sally, to New Mexico with

Healing and Transforming

a group of midlife women who were moving into their Third Act and searching for an identity that would give meaning and fulfillment to their new lives. We knew that in most Native American tribes women were honored as leaders in their culture and sacred figures in their spirituality. The goal for our group was to explore the sacred female figures, or goddesses, in Native American tribes of the Southwest, learning from them how we might enrich our own lives as women in our present society.

In our exploration, we soon saw that sacred female figures had many different functions and different names. But the one that stood out the most to me was a fascinating goddess known as Grandmother Spider or Spider Woman. Old, wrinkled, spidery and ancient beyond reckoning, Grandmother Spider is believed to live in *Shipop*, the underground world. It was she who led humans from one world to the next as they moved toward progressively higher levels of consciousness. And it was she who instructed humans in the meaning of "Right Relationship" and showed them how to live in peace and harmony with each other. She also taught them the practical skills of weaving, pot-making, and planting, plus she gave them the sacred rituals that bring them light and warmth. With her help, they became "true human beings."

Grandmother Spider was seen as the Creator, or Transformer, who manifests reality out of her own substance. She is the mystical power that created all the creatures in the universe and drew them together with her beautiful, silver webs. Her message was that we all are part of one universe, and therefore part of each other, forever connected by Grandmother Spider's deep love and infinite wisdom.

As part of our group's goal, we decided that each of us would focus on one goddess, study the meaning of that goddess and take it on as our self-image throughout our trip. Since I was the oldest of the group and a grandmother, I was given the role of Grandmother Spider, and in keeping with Native American tradition, I was also expected to be the wisest, most powerful one of the group. I laughed and shared their enjoyment of this, but underneath, I was uncomfortable with that title. I wanted to think of myself as a peer, not as an old woman. And I also didn't feel comfortable in the role of "wise elder."

Ever since the trip, I noticed many other women with no knowledge of Grandmother Spider began treating me as the older, wiser one. I continued to feel uncomfortable with that role because I knew that there were many things I did not know, and I couldn't see myself as wise.

But that day when I was driving home from my office and thinking back on all this, I suddenly realized that, like it or not, I was Grandmother Spider to slightly younger women who were looking for guidance in this new stage of their lives. And so, with a deep breath, I allowed myself to absorb that role. If it was given to me, I would receive it with grace and humility and do my best to guide not only other women, but also myself, my own Inner Child. Grandmother Spider became my new self-image.

And so it is for each of us as we go through our New Third Act. To be authentic with ourselves, we must let go of self-images that no longer serve us and take on the self-images that suit us at this point in our lives. As we live our new roles, we become stronger, clearer, and more comfortable with our new selves.

Loss and Grief

As discussed in Chapter 11, by the time we have reached the Third Act, we all have experienced loss. It is important to acknowledge these losses, grieve them, and let them go, so we can move on and fully live our present lives.

This applies to all losses, even those that seem small or insignificant. For example, the loss of a favorite childhood toy or a treasured book may seem too small to count, while the loss of youthful hopes and dreams may not even be thought of as losses. Such losses must at least be recognized and given their due.

Then there are the really big losses, such as the loss of a child, a dearly loved spouse, or family member. These losses are so painful that we often avoid facing them; we repress their memory, deny their importance, or convince ourselves that we have gotten beyond them when we have not. Such losses can throw us into shock for months or even years. Gradually they may recede, but even so, they remain with us, leaving blocks of frozen energy that we dare not approach and therefore cannot use in our present lives.

Grieving is the healing process that unthaws our frozen places and restores the energy to our present lives. A circular, non-linear process, grieving is best thought of as a spiral constantly circling back on itself as it moves forward into the future. Often, an event in our present life is the trigger that sends us spiraling back through painful memories. Thus, we may revisit our losses over and over, but with each visit the pain may become less intense and more easily released than in the past.

Grieving requires patience. It is not intended to erase past losses; it is a process of integrating them by gradually absorbing them into our expanding psyches where we experience them with less pain and a more mature perspective. Grieving is also an individual process. Each person revolves through the stages at his or her own pace. There is no proper time frame, regardless of what social mores or customs of the time may dictate.

There are many ways to describe the stages that we experience in our grieving cycle. The following seven steps are not absolute, but can be thought of as a general guide to lead us through our own unique paths of healing.

Acknowledging. The first step in the grieving process is to acknowledge the losses we have experienced and the impact they have had on our lives. These include not only the loss of friends and loved ones who have passed away or are no longer in our lives, but also other losses such as healthy bodies that can be taken for granted, freedom from physical pain, the hopes and dreams of youth, seemingly unlimited futures with no thought of mortality, and social roles that provided us with identity and purpose, among others.

Grieving. Once acknowledged, the second step is to grieve our losses. Grieving involves emotions—identifying them, feeling them, and expressing them in the way that feels right. Growing up in an emotion-phobic culture, many of us never learned how to grieve. We may even have learned *not* to grieve, or at least, not to show our grief.

But grieving is a central part of healing our losses. All of our losses produce a complexity of emotions, such as sadness, anger, anxiety, relief, fear, loneliness, and despair. Lessening our grip on these emotions allows them to flow from us in whatever form we choose—talking, drawing, writing, dancing. We can cry, sob, yell, scream, rage, laugh, or moan. The more deeply felt, the better. In this manner, we drain the energy around our losses, allowing the body to know at the deepest level that it is okay to release its tension, freeing us to be fully present to our current lives.

Witnessing. Grieving in the presence of a caring witness who listens in a supportive, non-judgmental manner has many benefits. It validates our feelings, allowing a full expression of our pain without self-blame or condemnation. Moreover, taking in supportive feedback from others offers us additional perspectives through which we can see our losses. In addition, it supports our ability to become loving witnesses to ourselves, which is ultimately what we must do to fully release our pain and gain a deep understanding of the meaning of our grief.

Comforting. Following naturally from witnessing, comforting means to receive support from others in an active manner through what is offered and shared. A warm hug is a classic mean of support, and even simple words conveyed with genuine empathy, such as "I understand," can be extremely comforting. Comforting from another person helps us to heal our pain. We no longer feel alone in the world; another soul shares our path and cares about us. As we heal, we discover healthy ways to comfort ourselves, too.

Accepting. As we begin to heal and regain our strength, we may discover ourselves relaxing into a sense of acceptance and forgiveness. We no longer need to hold onto the painful memory or the many emotions attached to it. We can accept and forgive. Please note this does not mean that we condone any transgression or abuse we may have suffered or relieve the other person of responsibility. Rather, it means that we no longer need to carry the pain inside us. Relieved of that burden, we can move on with our lives. We remember, but we no long suffer.

Transforming. This is where the magic begins. Freed from our energy-devouring grief, we find that the process has transformed us. We realize what we did not dream possible before grieving—our pain contained a gift. Not only do we have a new perspective on life—one that we were incapable of before our voyage through the path of grief—we discover that we are more caring and compassionate toward others and, perhaps more importantly, toward ourselves. It enriched our soul and showed us a new way to live.

Giving. In our healed state, we offer ourselves to others, supporting them through the difficult terrain of their suffering and teaching them what we have learned through our own experience. Together, witnessing and comforting for another requires we be able and willing to stay present through descriptions of deep and terrible pain without abandoning the griever. Through this process, we help the grieving person hold her pain, either literally or metaphorically, until she is strong enough to hold it herself.

Now we choose to use our transformed pain to help. We become the wounded healers of the world, empathic teachers who use what we have learned from healing ourselves to help others heal themselves. Together, we let go of the pain from the past and move forward toward a better life as a different person on a higher level.

Reflect:

Who are you now? What is your self-image, and how do others see you?

What impact have your losses had on your life? Which ones have you not fully grieved?

What gift have you discovered as you grieved and released the pain?

What have you learned about yourself as you witnessed and comforted another through the grieving process?

Simplifying and Strengthening

After we have let go of issues from the past that were standing in the way of our personal growth, we take a look at what needs to be done to live fully in our present life. Two tasks need to be addressed before we can move forward with personal growth in our New Third Act. The first task is to simplify our lives, so we can create space for new growth to occur. The second task is to strengthen body, mind, and spirit, so we can embrace the new energy that flows into us.

Simplifying

By the time we reach the New Third Act, most of us have accumulated many things that were important to us in our past, but are no longer necessary or wanted in our present life. Picture the many objects in your home, office, and surroundings that you haven't used in years, but you have not had the energy or gumption to take on the task of sorting, organizing, and hauling to donate or discard. Like all those books you've read and no longer want, but there they are taking up space and gathering dust. There's clothing that no longer fits or is totally out of style, and there are trinkets of all sorts that were perfect for past occasions but are no longer meaningful or useful. There's china and many other sentimental items passed down through generations, and, even though you don't like—perhaps never liked!—"Grandma's china," you can't bring yourself to give it away to somebody that might actually value it. We all have basements, attics, or storage units full of stuff that we or someone else *might* need someday, or things not important enough to live with, yet our hearts just can't seem to let go of.

So, you're stuck with all this clutter. You're not alone; there are many other women out there moving into their New Third Act who struggle to rid themselves of unwanted stuff and simplify their lives. Throughout my life, I have managed to accumulate many objects and found myself surrounded by piles of stuff I don't want but couldn't find the energy to get rid of.

Simplifying and Strengthening

One day I stopped at my favorite Macy's to do a little shopping, even though that's really the last thing I needed to do at that time. As was my habit, I walked in the side door right in front of the jewelry counter. I paused to take in the full vista in front of me—the racks and racks of sweaters, slacks, dresses, and jackets, and in the distance, the displays at my favorite make-up counter, Clinique. Then, of course, in the middle of the store, there are the familiar escalators inviting me to the second floor and feast on glittering china, deluxe housewares and linens, fancy luggage, and plush furniture. All delighted me as I imagined using it in my home.

Then all of a sudden, I stopped in my tracks as a wave of emotions washed through me. I realized at a gut level I really, really didn't want to be in that store—or any store, for that matter. The feelings were so strong that I almost screamed out "I hate everything in this store!" But I contained myself and left.

All the way home I laughed, thinking of what would have happened if I hadn't contained that scream. I imagined the possible headline in the local newspaper: "Psychologist Goes Berserk Shopping At Macys".

It was then I realized I needed something different in my life—something deep, yet basic—something that more "things" could not satisfy. Although I did not know what this something different was, I knew that I was tired of things and wanted to be washed clean of them.

When I got home, I immediately started sorting through my clothes, and while doing that, I made a vow to myself. I promised that, from then on, any time I bought a piece of clothing, I would give away one from my closet. Then I eyed my next "victims"—the many books sitting on shelves through the house. The same vow applied to them. When I got a new book, I gave away one from my collection. And after the books came the trinkets and jewelry passed on from Aunt Elsie after she died at the ripe old age of 106.

Although I recognized that de-cluttering is an ongoing process, I immediately began to experience its benefit. I felt lighter, fresher, and more open to the events of my life. I imagined I felt something like a snake must feel as it slowly molts, shedding its old skin, and slipping away smoothly on its fresh new one, leaving the old, unneeded skin behind. Something heavy had been lifted off me, and I felt free to new possibilities.

De-cluttering my surroundings allowed me to think more clearly, focus on what I love, and do what is really important to me at this stage of my life. My life became solidly built around three things I love: my music, my relationships, and my work. I play the piano an hour a day, keeping my fingers strong and my technique up to snuff, so I can enjoy the touch of my fingers on the keyboard and the beautiful tones of Bach and Chopin on my beloved Steinway. I schedule time on a regular basis to be with my family and close friends. I also write and counsel, sharing with other women the wisdom I have gained over the years, so they, too, can find the fulfillment they need and deserve in their New Third Act.

Clutter in our surroundings and clutter in how we manage our lives definitely indicates we have clutter in our minds. Our external lives reflect our inner lives. So, when we de-clutter our external lives, we free our minds to think clearly, to open more space within ourselves for personal growth, and to focus on how we want our lives to be.

Strengthening

When we reach midlife, everything changes. We may find that our bodies begin to make themselves heard in a new way, our minds do not operate as smoothly as they did a few years ago, and our spirits may lose the zest for life that we had enjoyed throughout our youth and early adulthood. Our bodies, minds, and spirits that we once took for granted now need our prime attention.

As we move into midlife, we need to strengthen ourselves in new ways. We must take steps to care for our bodies, stimulate our minds, and feed our spirit on a regular basis. We each must decide for ourselves how to incorporate these steps into our lives.

Body. As previously shared, I was confronted with physical problems that I had never faced before early in my midlife. First came a heart hammering out of control, and after that, a period of frightening numbness that spread through my arms and legs and even up into my neck. With good medical help and hard work on my part, I overcame these problems and became conscious of my body in ways I never was before. I developed a regimen of daily practices that has strengthened my body and helped me stay healthy: daily walking and exercising, staying on a healthy diet, drinking lots of water, joining classes in tai chi and yoga, getting plenty of rest and sleep, and treating my body to a frequent massage. Taking care of my body has become a priority in my life.

And I am not alone. I have many women friends in midlife and beyond who, like me, place taking care of their health as number one in their lives. My good friend, Anita, has faced difficult health issues over the years—migraines, allergies, high blood pressure, and thyroid problems. She has learned to deal with them through

Simplifying and Strengthening

healthy eating, the right medication and supplements, and most of all, lots of exercise. Knowing how to handle health problems has become especially important in the last ten years of her life when she has been forced to cope with extreme emotional and physical stress. In 2002, Anita's husband, Paul, was diagnosed with cancer. After two and a half years of battling the cancer with Anita and her son, Bill, as the only caretakers, Paul died. Then, as if that were not enough, five years later, Anita's daughter-in-law died from injuries sustained in an accident, leaving Bill and his three children with no one to turn to but Anita. Anita's dreams of a long, restful retirement went down the drain. She was now the "mother" of three school-age children, all of whom were struggling with the loss of their mother and needing emotional and physical care. Amazingly, Anita managed to do this, and at the same time continued to look strong and healthy for her age. When I asked her how she did it, she answered without hesitation, "Exercise!" Her regimen includes walking, aerobics, swimming, and weightlifting, over 20,000 pounds twice weekly. And she has the muscles to prove it!

Of course, every woman's body is unique, and how you deal with your physical issues is your own decision. But the thing to remember is that, for all of us, beginning with midlife and continuing for the rest of our lives, keeping our bodies as healthy as possible should be our number one priority.

Mind. One of the problems of aging, and clearly the one we all dread, is dementia of some sort, primarily Alzheimer's disease. Although this is generally a disease of later life, it can begin in our fifties or sixties, and in any case, most of us are keenly aware of any symptoms that suggest a possible first step toward Alzheimer's. This was certainly true for me because, as I shared in Chapter 11, my father had dementia for the last five years of his life. Although it was never diagnosed as such, he had symptoms very much like Alzheimer's. And since I was the child in the family that was most like my father, I naturally feared that when the time came I would share his fate.

Sure enough, as I moved through my sixties and into my seventies, I began to have problems with my memory. Over and over, I found myself walking determinedly down the hall to my bedroom, only to find when I got there I hadn't the slightest idea what I came for. And the only way I could remember was to go back to the room where I started, stand and look around, and suddenly it would come back to me—oh yes, I came back for my phone, or my cup of tea, or my blue house slippers,

Simplifying and Strengthening

or yesterday's newspaper, or—I could go on and on. The biggest problem was keeping track of my glasses. I have often caught myself searching for my glasses when they were hanging on the neck of my blouse, sitting on the top of my head, or, the very worst, perched on my nose the whole time.

In the last couple of years, I began to have problems recalling words or names when I needed them. In the middle of a conversation with a friend or when I have something important that I want to say to a client, I find myself stuck in the middle of "verbal nowhere." I know what I want to say, I can *feel* it, but I just can't bring it clearly to mind. It's extremely frustrating and sometimes embarrassing. Of course, the words that I want come to me later, so I know they're stored in the brain somewhere, but I just can't retrieve them when I want them.

All of this really scared me until I found that many people of my age, my husband included, complained of the same problems. Well, I thought, we couldn't all be in the early stages of Alzheimer's, so I began to explore what is known about aging and dementia. I found that what I was experiencing was part of normal aging. However, it is important to do what we can to keep our brains healthy. This includes regular exercise, a healthy diet, and good social connections, as well as keeping our minds active in many ways like reading, involved in games like crossword puzzles, continuing our education, learning new skills, and being creative. My personal brain-stimulating program includes these, and I also write and play the piano on an almost daily basis.

To keep your mind sharp, you have to use it by finding and engaging in ways to keep your brain tuned in and healthy. This keeps you ready to partake in the fulfilling experiences available to us in this stage of our lives.

Spirit. Spirit is the part of us that transcends both body and mind bringing joy and meaning to life far beyond any activity from the everyday. Some look to religion to find their spirit, but many experience their spirit in other ways. These experiences feed our spirits by lifting us above the daily routines and making our lives meaningful and worthwhile.

There are many ways to feed our spirits. One beautiful example came from my good friend, Kelly. We are both music lovers and find as many opportunities as we can to enjoy good music together. One evening as we were leaving the concert hall after experiencing a magnificent concert by the Atlanta Symphony Orchestra and Chorus, Kelly told me a story about her husband, William, who died several years before. They had

Simplifying and Strengthening

attended many symphony concerts together, and one evening after an especially beautiful concert, William stood up and pronounced, "My soul is adjusted!" From that day forward after every great music experience, Kelly stands up, stretches her arms toward the heavens, and exclaims, "My soul is adjusted!" Some people may be confused by the words "soul" and "adjusted" instead of "spirit" and "fed," but personally, I love that expression and share her feelings. And Kelly says that when she hears great music, she feels a deep shift in her body—a "soul adjustment"—that fills her with warmth and joy. In other words, great music feeds her spirit.

When I asked my good friend, Margaret, who for twenty years as a spiritual director helped clients learn how to live rich lives, "What feeds your spirit?" she closed her eyes, bowed her head, and thought for a while.

"My spirit is enriched in many ways. My dear friends, those who truly 'get me,' can sing my melody when I've forgotten the tune. My faith. My companionship with other women seeking to live generous and full lives. My commitment to a healthy lifestyle through exercise, eating well, and getting enough sleep, and this is important because spirituality is embodied. And if I neglect myself physically and don't take care of myself in concrete ways, my spirit becomes forlorn. And although

I'm basically an indoor person, nature feeds my spirit, especially in the spring or fall when the world is so alive with the beauty of creation. I can't resist being out in it.

"Another thing that feeds my spirit is reading wonderful books and discussing them with curious people. Books by Barbara Kingsolver or Ann Patchett, and works of non-fiction by thoughtful women who share their struggles and have made it to the other side, women like Sue Monk Kidd. For me there's nothing as satisfying as an afternoon sitting by an open window with a book that helps me name and claim my experience as a woman. Good therapy also feeds my spirit by providing a place to go and untangle knots, be challenged when I wish to grow, be comforted when the roof falls in, and be sustained through a wilderness time. And most of all, there's that moment when I'm sitting with a client and I feel the façade drop away and the real person emerge, communing at that deeper level where we are just two people in the same boat, helping each other across."

Perhaps you feed your spirit through practicing meditation; gardening; nurturing close, loving relationships; holding a newborn baby; visiting aquariums and zoos; volunteering at a pet rescue facility; rafting on a river or combing a beach; traveling; marching with people who all feel strongly about the same cause; attending poetry readings and the theater; touring museums, galleries and architectural wonders; painting, sculpting or creating with fiber and fabrics; writing your memoir or a fictional work... The list of experiences that lift and feed our spirits is infinite. Full participation is the important element, because in the New Third Act, nourishing our spirits is central to our search for meaning and fulfillment.

Reflect:

When you release some personal items, can you feel the freedom in your mind? What do you now have room to explore?

In what ways do you nurture your body? How can you enhance this?

How do you stimulate your mind? What are ways you've witnessed others doing this? Try one.

How do you feed your spirit? What is one new approach you can try to enrich this?

17

Discovering Your Inner Observer

Reaching fulfillment in the New Third Act requires that we live authentically. When we were young, we had a clear connection to our inner self, which allowed us to live genuinely. We knew what we felt and what we wanted, and we acted on that. However, over the years, pressures of family and culture forced us to shift our focus from what *we* wanted to what *others* wanted. We learned to direct our attention outside ourselves, and in the process, we weakened the connection to our inner selves. We lost much of our authenticity and thus weakened the life force that energizes and gives meaning to life.

When we reach the New Third Act, we find ourselves facing a new reality. The old structures that shaped our lives throughout our adult years are no longer satisfactory. Inside ourselves, we feel a strong urge to live the life we were meant to live, to make the difficult but exciting choice to grow. To do this, we must reconnect to and express the inner self we knew as a child, but this time with full consciousness and the broad perspective of many years' experience. It is this newly conscious authentic self that will guide us through the New Third Act of our lives. This is our Inner Observer.

The Inner Observer is a neutral part of the mind that stands outside of our thoughts, feelings, and body sensations, observing them clearly as we experience them. Nothing about our experience is changed. We continue to have the same thoughts and feelings; we simply add the element of awareness. We know what we're doing as we are doing it. Of course, since we are now aware, we can also choose to think, feel, or act differently if we wish. It is important to learn how to recognize the Inner Observer. Following are ways this occurs through our thoughts, feelings, and body.

Thoughts

Are you aware of the many thoughts that go through your mind every day? Our minds are constantly busy churning up thoughts; however, most of the time we are not consciously aware of them. If you use your Inner Observer to tune into your mental chatter, you will discover what your mind is up to.

You may see that your thoughts often stray far from what you are doing at that particular moment. In other words, you aren't really present. Or, you may realize that many thoughts recur over and over, forming habitual patterns of thinking in your mind. We may be shocked to observe how many of our thoughts are negative, including both self-criticism and replayed judgments from others.

These thoughts may unconsciously poison our system, damage our self-esteem, and weaken the flow of life energy. Many of these patterns were established in childhood and have gone unchanged for years. We need to examine each of these patterns, discarding those that are either inappropriate for our present lives or have become obstacles to our growth. Conscious awareness helps us eliminate these thoughts. The Inner Observer assists us in this process in many ways. Here are three ways I use which may be helpful to you.

Adopt a meditation practice. Take time each day to sit or lie quietly and observe the thoughts that flow through your mind. Don't stop the thoughts; just notice them, and let them go. Practice allowing your

Inner Observer to stand off to the side, watching without judgment. Over time, you will come to know your patterns of thought, as well as how to quiet your mind and open an inner space for new learning.

Periodically during the day, observe what is going through your mind. Is your mind present, or has it wandered somewhere else? Are you off in the future, planning your day, or worrying about something that may never happen? If you're like me, that's exactly what your mind is doing most of the time. Like me, you can learn to gently bring yourself back to the present. And to help myself in this process, I try to set aside a special time every day for worrying, planning, making lists, and so forth. That way my mind can be more at peace for the rest of the day.

Look for patterns in your thinking that may keep you stuck in your usual way of living. Are these patterns worth keeping? If not, open up to new options and find the courage to break the old ones. Be creative. Think outside the box. Do something different.

Feelings

When we were growing up, most women were taught to value rational thinking and discount our emotions, which in our culture are viewed with suspicion and sometimes disdain.

Moreover, in our culture, emotions are considered the province of women, and therefore, inferior and somewhat troublesome—definitely not a source of *reliable* information. We are told that decisions in life are to be made rationally with those distracting emotions kept clearly out of the picture. For most of us, the phrase "you're getting emotional" means you're sounding like a woman—heaven forbid!—and you're definitely on the wrong track.

As a result, we learn to hide our emotions, especially the ones other people wouldn't care for like those thought of as dark emotions, such as anger, fear, grief, or despair. But in doing so, we lose valuable information that can guide us to more meaningful and fulfilling lives.

Yet our feelings are a valuable source of information about the state of our well-being—what is happening to us and what we need to do about it. To avail ourselves of this important information, we must reconnect with our emotions and learn to express them appropriately. The Inner Observer can help us do this.

Become aware of your emotions. If you are aware that you are feeling something, locate that feeling in your body. What part of your body holds that feeling?

Is your stomach churning? Are you short of breath? Are your palms sweaty or your muscles tight? Are you tapping your fingers or twitching your feet? Asking yourself these questions on a regular basis helps you connect to your body and develop emotional sensitivity.

Name and describe your emotions. Are you happy, sad, angry, frustrated, or fearful? Is that feeling strong, faint, comfortable, painful, strange, or familiar? You may discover that what you thought was one emotion was in reality several emotions meshed together. Sorting these out and recognizing each of them increases emotional clarity.

Learn to dialogue with your emotions. When you are aware that you're feeling something, what is that feeling telling you about yourself? What do you need, want, or not want? What should you do? Emotions deliver information from our bodies to our minds where we can think about these issues and decide what steps to take. The Inner Observer helps us to connect with our emotions and act consciously rather than automatically and unconsciously.

Develop emotional tolerance. To take charge of our lives and gain inner strength, we must call on the Inner Observer to help us stay aware and open to all of our emotions, no matter how strong or painful they may be. This is especially true in the New Third Act when our lives no longer have the clear roles and external guidelines that we relied on in the past. We must learn to tolerate the anxiety that is aroused when we plow new ground, or when we take that first step off the cliff, trusting the wings of our inner knowing to carry us safely to the new life. We must openly acknowledge and forgive our past mistakes, so we can move forward into our lives with an open heart. And we must learn to tolerate the guilt that we feel when we choose to focus on our *own* growth rather than to continue being constant caretakers of others as most of us were taught to do.

Body

In the past, we believed that the mind and body were separate, having little to do with each other. We now know this is incorrect. In fact, our bodies and minds might be described as one big communication machine. Many now refer to the mind/body as a cohesive unit, not a duality. We now know that our minds exist not only in our brain, but also throughout our bodies. Bodily organs, like the heart, have their own "minds" and continuously send messages to the brain and other organs of the body. To do this, they use not only our nervous and endocrine systems, but also the many energy paths, or meridians, which wind through our bodies.

Of course, the body's language is not verbal. It is an organic, nonverbal language we experience as body sensations. These come in many forms, such as pain or pleasure, as well as nausea, dizziness, stiffness, and tremors, among others. These sensations are messages informing us about the state of our body, and therefore of our whole being. Most of us have not learned to be sensitive to body sensations, much less view them as a form of language.

However, by using our Inner Observer, we can learn to tune into that language and understand what our hearts, stomachs, uteruses, or other organs are communicating to our brain. When we listen to them, we can learn whether we are sick, in physical danger, or in need of healing. We can also sense the ebb and flow of our energy, what invigorates or drains us, when we need to take a rest, and much more. All these body sensations are trying to get our attention. Using the Inner Observer, rather than denying and avoiding these sensations, we can treat them as "friends," our nonverbal guides to health and well-being.

Practice tuning into your body on a daily basis. Consider doing this at night before going to sleep or in the morning upon awakening. Go through your body and feel your sensations. Check in with all your major body organs. What do you feel?

Be aware when your body sends you a nonverbal message. Where is it coming from? What is it saying? Is the message a symptom alerting you to a condition that needs your attention?

Notice your level of energy. Think back on the day, and ask yourself what energized and what drained you. What can you do about that? Can you do energy check-ins throughout the day? Notice when you are energized, as well as when you are tired.

Make a regular practice of engaging in mind/body activities. These include yoga, tai chi, massage, and a variety of energy work, for example. These activities help you relax, open your body, and tune into its valuable messages.

Ask questions of your body. What do I need that I don't have in my life? What do I have in my life that I don't need? What can my body teach me about the direction that my life should take?

Our Inner Observer helps us live authentically. We can *act* rather than *react*. We can become conscious of our choices and make them intentionally. And since the Inner Observer is neutral—that is, non-judgmental—it also helps us become less critical and more accepting of ourselves. We can love ourselves as the real human beings we *are* rather than as the "perfect" women we are told we *should* be. And as an added bonus, our new self-love flows over into compassion for others, leading us to a more deeply satisfying life.

Reflect:

What are your thoughts, feelings and body sensations as you discover and embrace your Inner Observer?

What times and routines work best for you to observe? Can you adapt and remain committed to these as your life improves?

Through sharing with other women, have you discovered new practices and ideas on this internal process?

18

Silencing the Inner Critic

By the time we get to our New Third Act, many of us may realize that we are not living the life we wanted or dreamed we would have at this point. Often, our first response to this realization is to look for something or someone to blame. We may look outside ourselves, blaming circumstances, just plain bad luck, or other people—spouses are a favorite target. Or, as is typical for women, we may point the finger inward and blame ourselves.

For most of us, placing the blame on others or outside events is easier. It relieves us of disturbing inner conflicts by allowing us to view ourselves as blameless victims of circumstances beyond our control. *We* are "good," and *they* are "bad." While many of us were truly victims as children, we no longer need to live that role as adults. We now have the power to choose to avoid or leave a bad situation, or to stand our ground and fight back. Not that it's easy. If we were victimized as children, we may learn to be helpless, failing to recognize obvious escape routes or to act on them even when we see them. Or in self-defense, we may model the behavior of our oppressors and become victimizers of others.

However in most cases, with hard work, determination, and help—something we all need—we can extract ourselves from the victim role. For our personal growth, it is essential that we do this. Otherwise, we remain helpless and fail to develop our talents or fulfill the promise of our lives. Meanwhile, with unexpressed anger eating at our guts, we can cause untold damage to our health while siphoning valuable energy that could otherwise fuel our personal growth. In addition, to justify our position as victims, we are often forced to distort reality, leading us to erroneous conclusions and unhelpful, even self-destructive, actions. Instead of living the life we want, we find ourselves trapped and frustrated in an unfulfilling situation.

Blaming ourselves can be even more disabling than blaming others. Often, we feel helpless and victimized, paralyzed by inner conflict. We may feel torn as we are both the blamer and the object of the blame. We see ourselves as "bad," while at the same time we resist that label. If on the surface we passively consent, then underneath we rebel; or if we choose to rebel openly, underneath we doubt ourselves. Unable to act with personal authority, our choices lack conviction and our actions are ineffective or self-destructive. As long as the conflict broils inside us, we can never be fully empowered.

Why does self-blame have such a profound influence on our lives? The answer is that the blaming voice in our heads is the internalized voice of messages from our childhood. They were passed to us, intentionally or not, by our parents and other authority figures, as well as by siblings, friends, peers, and the character of the culture in which we live. And as adults viewing the world through the distorted lenses we inherited from our childhood, we often find ourselves choosing friends and partners who continue to reinforce the blaming messages. We have developed our own "Inner Critic."

Once developed, our Inner Critic follows us through our days commenting, scolding, pointing out our "mistakes" and "stupidities," and otherwise undermining our lives. Most of this is entirely unconscious. But even when we are aware of the process, our Critic never feels like an alien being. After years of internalizing the Critic's messages, they now feel like our own thoughts. This fact, along with its deep roots in our childhood, gives our Critic the power to reach the core of our being. For example, when you think, "Why bother to try? I'll never amount to anything," you unconsciously reinforce a core message that says, *"I am defective."* Or when you think "Well, I certainly made a mess of that—as usual!" you reinforce the core message *"I am inadequate and incompetent."* Or with the thought "Why would somebody like *that* be interested in me?" the underlying core message is *"I am unlovable."*

The frequent presence of the Inner Critic in our minds leaves us more insecure and thus more likely to fall into the "people pleasing" mode. We know our own "flaws"—our Critic reminds us every day—but, in our naivety, we often convince ourselves that others have no flaws and are better, stronger, and more together than we. We believe the masks on others' faces, even though we know full well we wear one ourselves. And because we bought into our childhood messages about our own fallibility, we believe that those who gave us these messages are "good," and by extension, that other, similar people are also good, especially those with authority. Above all, we need to believe that somebody out there knows the answers, the "right way" to do things. We can't bear the thought that *nobody* knows, that maybe there isn't any "right way," and that maybe—just maybe—we have to find our *own* answers. That's just too scary to contemplate.

All of these issues become more important as we move into our New Third Act where achieving authenticity is essential if we are to live a satisfying life. To do this, we must gain clear access to our own internal voices and then develop the strength and courage to face our Inner Critic. But this is very difficult with the Inner Critic in charge. With its constant criticism, the Critic weakens our connection to our true inner voice— the source of our spontaneity, creativity, and power. It is clear, therefore, to live authentically we must disempower our Inner Critic and replace it with messages that affirm and empower us.

Disempowering our Inner Critic is not an overnight job. The process is gradual. It takes patience, practice, and commitment to free ourselves from this tyrant. The goal is not to totally eradicate the Critic's voice. We will always remember it. Rather, the goal is to weaken it and override it with positive messages. We learn to *recognize* and *contain* the critical voice while simultaneously opposing it with the voice of our true selves. The words of the Critic remain in our heads, but they lose their power. We say to ourselves, "Oh, there you are, my old Critic, popping up to deliver that tired old message. Thanks for sharing. Now go sit down." And we shuttle it away to another part of our brain while we go forward with our lives.

There are many ways to approach the task of disempowering the Inner Critic. The following guidelines may help you discover what ways work best for you.

Get completely familiar with the many messages delivered by your Inner Critic. Using your Inner Observer, carefully observe your Critic in many different circumstances. Observe the words it uses to convey its message. What is the core message underlying those words? Can you determine where those words originated? Mother? Father? Teacher? Notice the people or events in your present life that trigger the voice of the Critic. Ask yourself why these people or events have such power over you. What unhealed places inside you do they touch? Scan your body for emotions and physical sensations aroused by the Critic's voice, noting what you feel and where you feel it. What part of your body is involved? All of these practices will help you to increase your awareness and gain power over the Inner Critic. In the process, you may discover that simply being aware of your Critic is, in itself, a powerful factor in weakening it.

Caught in the act, so to speak, its critical message begins to lose its force.

Learn to override the power of the Inner Critic. In observing the Inner Critic, you may notice that when it speaks, it not only arouses feelings, but it also disrupts your natural path of action, causing you to feel helpless and doubt yourself. Without inner awareness, that's where most of us drop out. To avoid this, we must consciously choose to ignore the Critic and follow our initial inclination. That is not easy. The Critic does not yield its power gracefully. When you move against it, you can expect to feel an onslaught of guilt and shame, the Critic's most powerful weapons. You will feel torn and conflicted, and your self-determination will be tested. Moreover, as you begin acting on your true feelings, you will experience anxiety, sometimes severe. You are breaking the "rules," and for this, you believe you will be punished. Initially, all of this can be confusing and disheartening. It takes patience, courage, and determination, but eventually the power of your Inner Critic will weaken.

Discover and act on your authentic voice. As the Inner Critic weakens, your connection to your own inner voice will clarify and grow. You can facilitate this process by regularly incorporating certain practices into your life. In any situation in which you find yourself, especially when you are faced with a choice, make it a practice to ask yourself, "What do I really feel about this? What do I really want, and what do I really need?" Set aside daily quiet times for meditation and reflection. Listen to those nagging feelings of discontent that you typically ignore in order to discover their meaning as they may have important messages for you. Prime the pump of your creativity through journaling, painting, or other expressive activities. Talk with a coach or therapist. And, perhaps most important of all, surround yourself with supportive friends who share your journey and understand your struggles.

Observe the consequences. What works and what does not work? Take responsibility for your actions, but *never* blame yourself as that only strengthens the voice of the Inner Critic. Stay in the neutral zone of the Inner Observer and treat all outcomes as lessons—not *mistakes*, just *lessons*. From this perspective, you not only learn to discern your true inner voice, but also how to speak and act on your own behalf.

By following these guidelines, you will find over time that the many negative feelings such as guilt, shame, anger, and frustration—for so long the background noise to your life—will diminish. In its place will be peace of mind and general good feelings toward others. And best of all, you will experience the fulfillment of living an authentic life.

Reflect:

Who have you blamed outside of yourself for circumstances within your control? Can you claim and learn from your lesson while forgiving yourself?

Have you noticed a time when you placed yourself in the roll of the victim? How can you empower yourself to move forward?

When you recognize self blame, can you view this as the Inner Critic? Can you counteract these messages in a positive way?

19
Going Deeper

In the last two chapters, we focused on two aspects of our path of growth—the Inner Observer and the Inner Critic. The Inner Observer supports our personal growth. It is the neutral part of the mind that stands outside of our thoughts and feelings, observing them clearly without criticism, helping us become more conscious and make better choices in our life. The Inner Critic is an obstacle to our personal growth. It is the part of us, mostly unconscious, that blames and scolds us for almost everything that we do.

Now we focus on going deeper within ourselves and become conscious of the core messages that are obstacles to our growth.

Button, Button, Who's Got the Button?

When I was a child, we played a game that went something like this: Standing in a circle with one child in the middle, who was "It," we secretly passed a button from one child to the next until the "It" person yelled "Stop!" and pointed to one child in the circle. The designated child then opened her hands. If she had the button, she was "It" and exchanged places with the person in the middle. The object, of course, was not to get caught with the button.

As an adult, I realized that in the game of life, "buttons" are still important. We all have them, and nobody wants to get caught with one. Buttons are emotional hot spots. When somebody "pushes a button," this person touches an emotional hot spot, an unhealed place inside us where we are still vulnerable to unexpected injuries from the outside. To avoid being hurt, we devise numerous strategies to protect our "buttons." For example, we limit our lives by avoiding situations that might expose them; we become expert dodgers, dancing carefully around conversational subjects that might lead to one of our buttons. We build impenetrable shields to prevent others from reaching our buttons, or we use our precious life energy to bury them deep in our psyches where even we forget their existence—until somebody accidentally hits one.

Since most of these strategies were devised early in life, as adults we may have little awareness of them, much less of the nature of our buttons, leaving us vulnerable to unexpected and unexplained hurts. To develop personal strength, we must become conscious of our emotional hot spots and do the work of healing them. The more we heal, the stronger we become.

Our hot spots are core messages with roots deep within us. For years, we have repressed and denied them, but now we must become aware of them so we can heal them and grow into a fulfilling life in our New Third Act.

When we were one or two years old, far back before most of us can consciously remember, we were whole and complete human beings. But somewhere along the road as we passed through our developing years and encountered life's inevitable bumps and barriers, we lost parts of ourselves—or so we thought. Actually, we still have all our parts; they're just repressed.

Why did we repress parts of ourselves? Basically, we did it to survive. As human infants, we could not live without care or thrive without love. Studies have shown that infants raised in institutions where they receive adequate physical care but very little stimulation

The New Third Act

or interaction with adults—holding, cuddling, cooing, rocking, or looking into a human face that is smiling back at them—do not thrive as well as normal infants, sometimes sinking into a chronic malaise or depression that can lead to illness and even premature death.

As children, we quickly learn that there are parts of our personality that do not please our parents. When parents show their displeasure, children often experience this as a withdrawal of love, and while it is happening, they feel abandoned, rejected, alone, and afraid—sometimes even desperate. Think back on your own childhood. Can you remember times when Mommy or Daddy was angry and turned away from you or sent you to your room, and nothing that you could do would restore that contact until the magic moment when she or he was ready to take you back?

In Chapter 4, I discussed how my mother was a master at this. Whenever she was angry with me, she turned her back and refused to respond to anything that I said. Until she recognized me again, I was totally distraught. I felt fear, frustration, and sorrow, and underneath it all, a sense of overwhelming helplessness and vulnerability. For that moment, I no longer felt loved. To this day, I have a picture in my mind of me as a small child, crying, looking up at my mother's back as

Going Deeper

she worked at the kitchen sink, angry about something I had done. No matter how much I begged to be hugged and forgiven, she refused to respond until *she* was ready. And to this day, when someone is angry and cuts me off, I feel like that helpless child again, and I have to work hard to pull myself back into my adult self and deal with the problem on an adult level.

These moments in our childhood when we felt cut off and unloved might not always be expressed directly, openly, or as the result of anger. For example, we might overhear our parents make remarks that are hurtful to us, such as praising a sibling or another child for traits we do not possess, or not noticing, much less praising, when we do something well. Although our parents may not mean to hurt us, these moments can be very powerful. They can leave us feeling less valuable than other children, a feeling that we can—and often do—carry with us into our adulthood. We were wounded without consciously knowing it.

It is no surprise, therefore, that we learn to hide the "bad" parts of ourselves, allowing only the "good" parts to be seen. Over the years, this process generalizes. We learn to hide our "bad" parts not only from our parents but from other people as well—especially from adults who have authority over us. Ultimately, we even hide them from ourselves by burying the "bad" parts so deep inside us that they become unconscious.

By the time we start school, we have a heaping handful of buttons, and by the time we reach adolescence, both hands can't possibly hold them all.

At this point, it is important to note that the parts of us that get repressed are not necessarily "bad." They may be perfectly normal reactions, such as feeling or expressing anger, but anger was not allowed in our family. Or they may be potential strengths and talents, such as sensitivity and/or exceptional intuitive ability which the parents did not recognize or understand. These qualities, for whatever reason, made our parents uncomfortable and were therefore labeled as "bad." Normal anger could be seen as disobedience and sensitivity as over-reaction. As children, most of us believed our parents and dutifully tried to stuff these traits deep within us. To do otherwise would expose us to the dreaded loss of parental love. The real loss, however, is our conscious access to the natural feelings and special strengths that constitute our power, strengths that were transferred into emotional hot spots.

Nevertheless, the process of repression continues. We start school, hear negative messages about aspects of ourselves from teachers and other authority figures, and those become more buttons. Later, it's our peers that haunt us. We lie to ourselves and to others, stuffing more and more, as we strive to be like the cheerleader we admire, or the prom queen, or the sorority president, or, later as adults, the "perfect mother," for example. We are filled with buttons. We may even burst open on occasion, exposing our hidden side in unexpected and often uncontrollable ways much to our dislike and consternation, leading us to even more self-repression.

By the time we reach midlife, many women lose competence due to so many emotional buttons and are forced to reverse course and begin personal examination instead of trying to stuff more. Of course, we all know that some women do not do this, choosing instead to expend energy trying to keep those buttons repressed forever at any cost. Sadly, these women will often never know what they have lost.

For those of us who decide to go forward, we quickly discover that getting our repressed parts out and healed is not easy. Though the prospect is more than a bit frightening, the confluence of inner pressure and outer circumstances pushes us forward. Once begun and had a taste of authentic living, we discover we can't go back. We must retrieve these qualities for our conscious and intentional use. To do so, take a look at your relationships, body messages, and dreams. We are irresistibly drawn forward.

And so we fearlessly become "It," the person in the middle with others circled all around, but instead of trying to give our buttons away and hide within the line, we heal them and show our true selves. We soon realize what a burden we have carried all these years. Unbeknownst to us, in an effort to hold all that we have suppressed, we used much valuable energy that otherwise could have been used to power our present lives. And without all of our energy, we cannot experience our lives to the fullest nor cope well with the inevitable challenges of later life.

In addition, as long as parts of us were hidden, we were deprived of the possibility of fully knowing and developing ourselves. For example, we may have failed to notice how we inadvertently hurt others and therefore disrupted potentially good and rewarding relationships. Or we may not have recognized our intuitive ability or our sensitivity, and therefore failed to develop these strengths into actions that would reward us and help others. Because we repressed many of our thoughts and feelings, we could not see all the ways in which we blocked our growth, sabotaged our lives, and deprived others of the unique qualities that only we have to offer.

Uncovering and facing our buttons can be a difficult task. It requires all of the skills and strengths we have so far developed. Throughout this journey, we must expect frequent encounters with our Inner Critic and be prepared to maintain the neutrality of our Inner Observer. We must develop the courage to face what we see, to tolerate the emotions that are aroused, and to act on what we learn. Even though it may upset our comfortable lives, the result is worth it. We now have access to our strengths and our full energy. We can experience the joy and fulfillment that is open to us all in our New Third Act.

Reflect:

What behaviors and/or personality characteristics did your parents reprimand you for?

What happened to these behaviors? Did you repress them? If so, have you reclaimed and healed them?

What are some of the hidden qualities you have repressed? What surfaces for you right now? How does your inner voice guide you to develop them?

20

Claiming Our Feminine Strengths

As we learn to deal with our Inner Critic and allow our inner voice to communicate with us, buried lessons rise for observation, healing, and re-energizing. Some of these, if not many at the root, may be anchored in gender. Growing up female in a world mostly dominated by men affects many of us. These issues can hold us back from attaining many of our sought after dreams and goals.

From the time I was a child, I sincerely believed boys were better than girls. As I grew older, I told myself I left that childish belief behind, but underneath, I knew it was not that simple. I was confused and conflicted on the whole issue. I resented men for their power and elevated position in society, but at the same time, I admired them, looked up to them for strength and leadership, and spent much time and effort trying to please them. Even though I tried to convince myself I was as strong and valuable as any man, I didn't really believe it.

It was only after I reached the New Third Act and began working with the deep issues of my life that I understood how that belief began, then healed and let it go to claim my own feminine strengths.

When I was a young child, I loved stories of any kind, especially stories that told me about people's lives. I spent many childhood hours following my mother around the house as she dusted furniture and mopped floors begging her to tell me stories about when she was a little girl. If she was in a good mood, she would comply, and in that way I learned to see life through my mother's eyes. At the time, I did not realize how much her vision overlaid my own and how hard I would work in my later years to regain my own view of life.

As it happened, my mother idolized her father, George Hunter, and so many of her stories involved him. As a child, mother spent many hours working in the fields with her father. She saw him as a strong, upright man who, through hard work and wise management, kept his family afloat on their small farming income and still found time to love and appreciate his children. By contrast, she was ashamed of her mother, whom she saw as self-centered, childish, and lazy, more concerned with her own comfort than with the well-being of her children or cleanliness of her house.

My mother's proudest moment came when, as a young woman, she overheard a conversation between her father and a friend. The friend asked, "George, who's your favorite among your children?" Her father replied, "Oh, you know I don't pick favorites with my children." The friend coaxed a little more. Finally, her father said, "Well, you see that one a-goin' there? She's about the best." Of course, my mother was "that one a-goin' there," and she held on to that treasured moment for the rest of her life.

In my child's mind as I listened to these stories about my deceased grandfather, he became a mythical figure—an ideal person whose life was the model for the way I should live my life. And since he was a man, it followed in my mind that men were better than women. This belief was reinforced by many other stories my mother told me. My favorites were the stories about her teaching days like the one I mentioned earlier about when, as a young woman, she taught in a one-room school.

Every day, she rode her horse to school and single-handedly managed a room full of children, grades one through eight. I was fascinated about her many tales of the big, rough country boys in the school and how she, young and small-statured, nevertheless taught, maintained order, and won their respect. Time and again she told how ornery the boys were, but she always laughed when she told it. This led me to believe she thought they were cute and even admired them in a way. As I listened, I laughed along with her, but secretly I felt ashamed and inferior because I could not imagine myself being strong enough to do all that. George Hunter was proud of my mother, but he wouldn't be proud of me.

The most painful times for me were when my mother told me how she preferred teaching boys to girls. "Little boys were open and honest," she said, "but girls were sneaky." And my mother definitely didn't like sneaky! I guess being sneaky violated the strong sense of integrity she had absorbed from her father. Naturally, since I was a girl, I wondered if that meant she didn't like me or that she loved my brother more than she loved me. That was a scary thought because, more than anything, I wanted my mother to love me. I was always too afraid to ask that question directly, but inside myself, I quietly determined not to be like one of those sneaky girls Mommy didn't like. I would be like the boys—ornery, perhaps, but out in the open. Maybe then my mother would love me. And maybe then I would be as good as my brother who had the advantage of actually being a boy.

For his first three and a half years, Dick was an only child, the beautiful baby boy that my mother had always wanted and the apple of everyone's eye. That exclusivity ended when I was born, and Dick was forced to share the limelight with me. I suppose he was always a bit jealous and threatened by any attention I received, but that's something I didn't realize until much later. As a child, and for much of my life, I have always felt I was in Dick's shadow—the "also ran"—the one teachers pointed to, after raving about my brother's brilliance, and said, "And this one will do alright, too."

Dick probably didn't want a sibling at all, but if it had to be, he definitely wanted it to be a boy. Of course, I disappointed him simply by being a girl. From the first, Dick made it clear to me—and I bought into it because, as his little sister I believed everything he said—that being a girl was far inferior to being a boy. Everything around me seemed to prove this. Boys had more interesting lives. They were the heroes who went on great adventures, rode horses, fought battles, played ball, and became the doctors, dentists, lawyers, and leaders of the community. On the other hand, women, as far as I could see, stayed home taking care of children, cleaning the house, and cooking the meals, or if they worked outside the home, which was rare in those days, they were teachers, nurses, or secretaries. This wasn't very exciting compared to men's work.

Often in my imaginative play, I pretended to be a boy. During the day, I became the male hero—a cowboy riding my stick horse up and down Cypress Street chasing Indians on the high plains, a captain in the Royal Canadian Mounted Police dashing across the Canadian wilderness bringing villains to justice, or, dressed in my father's old World War I helmet, a soldier marching up and down the street in a victory parade for all to admire. And every night before bed, I ritually donned my brother's knickers and lace boots, and then I strutted around the bedroom trying to feel what it was like to be a boy. Dick thought this was funny as did my mother.

Of course, being a girl, I had fun playing "girl games" alone or with my girlfriend Peggie. We played house, cut out paper dolls, jumped rope, and dressed our "babies." When the older girls, Betty and Ruby, were around, we often played "dress up." With Peggy and me dressed as little girls and Betty and Ruby as grown-up women in high heels, we strolled proudly up and down the street for everyone to see. But best of all, I learned to tap dance like my idol, Shirley Temple, which was fun and got me lots of attention, especially when I danced to my favorite song "If You Knew Suzie Like I Know Suzie." Honestly, I can still tap some of this.

But even though I enjoyed playing with girls most of the time, I also played boys' games with my brother. Baseball was our favorite sport. Dick practiced with me on a regular basis, teaching me to hit, throw, catch fly balls, and field grounders. At some point, it was decided that I would become a shortstop and one day replace the famous Marty Marian of our beloved St. Louis Cardinals. I loved the idea, and it all seemed quite real. Underneath, though, I always knew that it was just a daydream and that, in the end, I would be disappointed. I was a girl, and everybody knew girls couldn't play baseball. Looking back on it now, I can laugh. How many women do you know that grew up wanting to play shortstop for the St. Louis Cardinals? But to this day, I cannot watch the movie *A League of Their Own* without crying for that wonderful, lost dream.

In spite of all my efforts, Dick and I both agreed that there was one fact that would forever prevent me from becoming a boy, a fact that proved the superiority of boys. It was our anatomy. Boys had a "dinkus," and girls didn't. Dinkus was our family name for penis. A dinkus was obvious and easy to see, and most of the boys I knew seemed very proud to have one. As far as I could tell, girls didn't have anything, or not much of anything. And anyway, whatever it was, it wasn't good enough to rate having a name.

I fervently wished that I could have a dinkus! Dick agreed, and my mother colluded with this hopeless wish. One scene was enacted a few times in my early childhood: Dick and I are standing in the living room, begging my mother to call the hospital and order the magic organ that would turn me into a boy. She plays along. Lifting the receiver of our old-fashioned phone, she pretends to give the number to the operator and talk to the hospital about my predicament. I wait excitedly, hoping that this time would be different—this time the hospital would deliver the coveted dinkus. But every time, the ending was always the same. Mother hangs up, turns to me and says, "Nope, sorry, the hospital can't do this," and then she bursts out laughing. To this day, I remember the disappointment and shame I felt at those moments. I couldn't really have a dinkus, and I couldn't really be a boy. It was all just a big joke—on me.

Eventually, of course, I came to accept that my body would never change genders—I was always going to be

Claiming Our Feminine Strengths

a girl. However, my struggle to feel equal to my brother continued. Even though I have had many accomplishments in my life, they never seemed quite as good as my brother's.

And so it went throughout my growing years. I continued to fight the belief that boys were better than girls, all the while denying that I held such a belief. But that denied belief stubbornly continued to lodge itself deep in my subconscious, causing problems in my relationships and my work throughout my teens and into my adult years. It was not until my New Third Act that I woke up and began the work of claiming my feminine strengths.

Many women like me have had experiences throughout their lives which left them feeling less valued than boys and men, whether this came from growing up in a family where males were valued more than females, or, in a general sense, what it means to be a woman in our society. Even for those of us who have reached midlife with many successes, these feelings may still lie deep within us, causing us to doubt our strengths. We must identify feminine qualities, examine how we can make these into our strengths, and determine how to use them for value in our lives and society.

In my work with women in the New Third Act, I found that most viewed feminine qualities as good, valuable at times, but soft, not muscular like those of men, so definitely not strengths. But as the women put it in the context of our current times, it became clear that feminine qualities, though soft, can be and often are valuable strengths.

Consider the quality of nurturing. It's true that both men and women can nurture, but clearly, it is women who do most of the nurturing, especially through the role of mothering. Nurturing is a strength, just as is its masculine counterpart of being a provider. In times before the 1970s, these were clear gender roles of the female and male, respectively. "Bringing home the bacon" was usually more touted as the man went out of the home and returned with the reward. "Frying it up in a pan" was simply seen as a task, one not as prized or valuable as earning. However, times have changed, and due to this shift, both qualities are viewed as necessary and strong.

Who was the parent that did most of the nurturing in your family? For some women, that was the father, but for most, it was their mother. Clearly, the ability to nurture another person is a feminine strength, but it's not mutually exclusive to women. Nurturing can come on many levels beyond raising children, too; it is a treasured life skill that transcends to communities.

Another feminine strength is compassion, which includes sensitivity, empathy, and the capacity to listen and truly hear another person. As a therapist, I am aware of both how important, as well as how satisfying, it is to listen deeply and compassionately. This not only allows my clients to open and release their deepest thoughts and feelings, but also, as I listen to them, it allows me to do the same for myself. We are both healed and strengthened. It's a pleasure to witness clients become clear on what they believed and how they want to live their lives.

Reflecting on women, both of past and contemporary times, allows you to view how valuable feminine strengths are for our society. Think about those who have mentored you and nurtured strengths which made you a stronger, more powerful woman. Also, consider those in the public eye and adopt them as role models, women like: Mother Teresa who spent her life helping the impoverished in India; Melinda Gates who guides much of the Gates fortune, providing funds for education and health support for people worldwide; as well as Eleanor Roosevelt, Hillary Clinton, Golda Meir, Eve Ensler, Jane Fonda, and so many others. All are fine examples of women who successfully built their lives around feminine strengths.

Both women and men have a variety of qualities encouraged in their lives, and some of these are shared by the genders. Still, each has counterparts considered as feminine/masculine—gentle/strong, intuitive/logical, responsive/initiating, cooperative/competitive, emotional/rational—but the lines are blurring. And as our world changes, women have greater opportunities. Women hold leadership roles in business and the military. Even in the medical field, women doctors have become more prevalent, as have male nurses.

Clearly, men have many valuable strengths, but as we can see, women also have equally valuable strengths. The goal is to identify those qualities that are true to you, especially those that were innate yet repressed or denied, and claim, elevate, and use them to enhance your growth.

Reflect:

As a child, did you have experiences that left your feeling less valued than men or boys? Have you become aware of these feelings and learned to heal and release them?

Which of the feminine strengths are your strengths? When and how do you use your strengths?

Who are women you know who help others by using their strengths?

21

Standing In Your Power

Standing in your power means that you are true to yourself in all you think, say and do.

Most often, when people speak of power, they mean "power over," the power that allows dominance over others and control of external events. But there is another form of power: inner power. This is the power of inner strength, the strength that allows us to follow our own truth regardless of what may happen or what others may think. Although less well known and harder to achieve, inner power is by far the greater power because it is not dependent on external events but only on the strength that lies within us. In the New Third Act, it is inner power we need to achieve.

When we stand in our power, we live according to our own beliefs rather than conforming to what others would have us think or do. But more than that, standing in our power means we live out of our *own* reality. We act according to how *we* see the situation, how *we* feel about something, or what *our* intuition and inner voice guides us to do. In matters of integrity, we do this, even when it conflicts with others views, socially accepted beliefs, or authoritative opinions.

Most opportunities to stand in our power are not huge events that happen only to special people on important occasions. They are part of everyday interactions among ordinary people. For example, we stand in our power every time we say "no" when we would ordinarily say "yes" to avoid hurt feelings; or when we ask the question we're dying to ask, in spite of our fear of appearing "stupid"; or when we tell someone what we really think, even though they may be angry with us.

Standing in our power does not mean we are blindly self-centered or lack compassion. We do not always insist on getting our way or refuse to acquiesce to others' opinions. Quite the opposite. Being thoroughly grounded in our own power allows us to have healthy dialogues with other people. From a grounded position, we are free to move in any direction. We may listen to and respect the viewpoint of the other person, but decide to stay with our original opinion. Or we may also decide to compromise, or even fully accept the view of another person as our own, if it aligns with our own authenticity. The essential point is that we choose consciously and in a manner that protects our integrity, as well as the integrity of the other person.

Thus, standing in our power is not merely an occasional act but a way of life. It allows us to live from our authenticity while allowing others to do the same.

Learning to stand in our own power is not easy. It requires personal strengths that take time and effort to develop. One of these strengths is the awareness of the Inner Observer, or the capacity to recognize what is really true for us, as opposed to what we have been taught to believe. This is often difficult because most people—especially women—grew up in situations that forced them to deny or repress their own reality. For example, when we expressed our opinions as a child, we were told that our interpretations were inaccurate or unacceptable. We learned not to trust our own experience and that the safest route was to refrain from expressing *our* reality until we checked it out with the "authorities." If our reality matched their reality, we could safely express it; if not, we suppressed ours and echoed theirs.

A problem in assessing our inner power is that we often cannot see our own strengths and weaknesses. One way to help ourselves with this is to look at the way we relate to other people. Who are the people that you especially admire? What strengths do you see in them that you don't see in yourself? Could it be that you have some of these strengths but are reluctant to "own" them? If you can't see any of the qualities in yourself, look again, because for the most part, the qualities that we see in others are those we actually possess ourselves, but we do not acknowledge or express, at least consciously. In other words, you may be denying your own inner power.

This exercise also works in reverse: Who are the people you most dislike or resent? Exploring this may also reveal denied aspects of yourself—qualities which you repressed out of fear or shame, but which may actually be potential strengths. In any case, denying any part of ourselves uses valuable energy, energy which otherwise could bolster personal strength and self-esteem.

Next, we must name our strengths and articulate our intimate experience to ourselves. Although our authentic feelings are still inside us through repression and lack of use, their signals have become weak and diffuse. Connecting with them requires skills that most of us did not learn in childhood where inner experience was not even acknowledged, much less talked about. We must learn to tune in more closely to our authentic feelings as they flit through our consciousness, sort them out, and determine what they mean. For feelings that have been deeply repressed, we must take time to patiently look into our selves, retrieve buried feelings, flesh them out, and allow them to develop and mature through active experience with the world.

Finally, we have to develop courage. It takes courage to honestly face our true selves. It also takes courage to stand in our power and speak our truth to others, especially if we know they might not agree with us. Past experience in dealing with the authorities of our childhood has left us convinced that we are less powerful than those who might oppose us, and we are fearful that speaking our truth will lead to rejection and painful criticism. Although intellectually we know we are adults, emotionally we feel like helpless children facing the anger of a disapproving parent. When we are in this space, we can't envision holding our own in a disagreement with powerful others. As a result, we don't speak up and lose the opportunity to stand in our power.

The good news is that it doesn't need to stay that way. Through patience and practice, you can develop courage. The secret is to take it a step at a time and avoid destructive self-criticism. Set the Inner Critic aside, then nurture and support yourself. Choose challenges that can be accomplished, and don't expect perfection. Fear is part of the process, but it lessens with each success. Remember the adage, "Speak your truth even if your voice shakes." Eventually your voice won't shake, and you'll find that you are living more and more from your authentic self.

Authenticity is important at all stages of life, but it is essential in the New Third Act. In the Second Act, we were given clear roles to play, personas which, to a certain extent, provided us with meaningful and respected lives. However, we can also hide behind these personas, becoming the good mother, perfect wife, or successful career woman. Few may realize that, at best, the persona expresses only part of who they are, and at worst, may entirely conceal the real person underneath leading to despair. But in the New Third Act, it is much more difficult to hide. Fulfillment at this stage of life requires that we become real.

Reflect:

Think of the three strengths required to stand in your power: awareness of inner experience, ability to articulate your feelings, and courage to act from your inner truth. Which of these is most difficult for you? What could you do to develop this strength?

Think of a situation in which you were not able to stand in your power. What aspects of the situation made it difficult for you? What strengths do you need to stand in your power in similar situations in the future?

Think of a recent situation in which you were able to stand in your power. What aspects of the situation made it possible for you to do that? What strengths did you use? How did you feel? What was the outcome?

22

Learning from Relationships

As we grow toward maturity in the New Third Act, our relationships with others are profoundly affected and, in return, profoundly affect our growth. It is in the context of relationships that we see ourselves most clearly. Relationships are our mirrors. If we allow ourselves to stay open and take in the "raw data," we learn valuable lessons that not only enhance our relationships but help us manage our lives more smoothly.

We have many relationships in our lives: parents, friends, partners, neighbors, co-workers, pets, and beyond that, any stranger with whom we might have a brief interaction. All can illuminate aspects of our lives, some more that others, but all in their own way. Three of our most important relationships are with family, partner, and friends.

Family

Of all our relationships, families are the most important teachers. Families give us our genetic heritage, and through their interactions with us as we are growing up, shape how we express that heritage. From families, we get our first self-concepts; we find out who we are from their point of view.

The earliest circle, the family, imprinted on our psyches when we are young and vulnerable, remains the most powerful. This is true even though the power and often the very existence of the family circle may be out of our awareness. The family circle influences and shapes all of our future circles, our ability to create our own circles, and our vulnerability to be drawn into others' circles.

In the First Act when we were young children, our lives revolve around us. We are the center of our own circle. In fact, from our point of view, we are the center of the universe. Of course, as we grow up and move through the inevitable socialization process, we discover much to our dismay that we are not the center of the universe. Most of the time we aren't even allowed to be the center of our own circle.

So, as time goes on, we come to see ourselves not as the center of our own circle, but as a part of another larger circle. For most of us, this is the family, and, in the beginning, this is primarily our mothers. Like spokes in a wheel, we learn to take our place as dependents who must please the central power in order to survive. We become pleasers and supporters of others. This is true for all, but especially for girls whose traditional social roles as adults place them in supportive roles. If we're "properly" socialized, we soon learn what is allowed and what is not allowed within that circle. That's when we begin stuffing parts of ourselves out of sight and shaping ourselves to fit into the circle we found ourselves born into.

Through our teen years, most of us are strongly pulled to join the circle of our peers, to be accepted and to find our place in the world of our own age group. The peer circle competes with the power of the original family circle, and this creates many of the problems and much of angst of adolescence. Eventually, most of us come to a rapprochement with this conflict and move on into a new, if somewhat shaky, circle of our own making. The Second Act has begun.

The New Third Act

One of our primary tasks as we grow through life is sorting out our first self-concepts from the self we develop as we go through life experiencing many different relationships and absorbing their feedback. Over the years, we begin to learn who we are and who we are not, as well as perhaps something of what we may become.

As stated earlier, my mother died when I was fifty-three years old, just beginning my path through midlife. After her memorial service, nine family members were crowded into our Aunt Elsie's room at the retirement center. Elsie was my mother's older sister. Earlier that week, Elsie had broken her shoulder in a fall and was unable to attend the service. Because of the fall, relatives who had come to support my mother felt obliged to divide their time between Mother and Elsie.

So here we all were back from the service and eager to tell Elsie about it, but we didn't get the chance. Instead, we were forced to focus attention on Elsie, who was holding court from her favorite chair in the center of the room, talking about herself and whatever interested her—but not about Mother.

"How typical," I thought. "Elsie always manages to be the center of attention; she can't even let Mother have her memorial." For years before my mother died, I had watched with frustration as she used up much of her energy dealing with Elsie, energy my mother could have spent taking care of herself and doing what she wanted to do. Little did I know that I would spend the next nineteen years of my life doing the same thing—unconsciously acting out an early childhood lesson that my happiness, and perhaps my very survival, depended on how well I pleased others.

Gradually during those years with Elsie, I became conscious of my own role in the relationship. I realized that I was reenacting my childhood role of accommodating and pleasing others. With my mother as the original teacher, transferring this role to her older sister had been easy and natural. This awareness allowed me to make different choices from my mother. I chose not to allow Elsie's demanding behavior disrupt my life. Implementing that choice was not easy, but over time I learned to set limits and expect respectful behavior from her. I didn't let her behavior get to me; I let go of my anger and accepted Elsie for Elsie. It was a difficult, but valuable, lesson.

That kind of teaching is important, but it's not the full story. What I'm describing is more subtle, indirect, and powerful. For example, it is in our families that most of us learn who we are, how valuable we are, what our flaws are, and what we need to change, or failing that, to hide from others. We also learn what the world is like: Is it friendly or dangerous? Whom can we trust, if anybody? Much of this information is taught indirectly and unintentionally through how we are treated, what we are told about ourselves, how our parents react to life, and what behaviors they model for us. In other words, our families give us our reality.

Furthermore, much of this reality is absorbed unconsciously, often at a pre-verbal level. As a result, it is so thoroughly etched in our minds that information to the contrary, received later in life, barely impacts us. Throughout the First and Second Acts of our lives, we continue to accept this reality, acting out our scripts in pursuit of happiness with a greater or lesser degree of success. It is only after life jars us into consciousness that we begin to question that reality and thus to open ourselves to new possibilities.

Partner

Please note: for the sake of brevity, I refer to our partner as a man, but the text applies equally well to relationships with same-sex partners.

When we are still in Act Two, thinking and behaving in the Act Two way, we envision life centered on a key relationship with a partner. When we finally meet him and form a relationship, our single life ends. Our lives as they were before we met him no longer exist, except in a very subsidiary fashion.

Although the "circle story" is never quite the same for men and women, at this point in life, it may really begin to diverge. For women, especially those of us who have been imprinted with the traditional view of life, our circles are never stable. In our feelings, if not our rational minds, our circle lacks a center. We envision life centered on a "key" relationship with a man.

In our minds, this man and his life already exist before we meet him. When—and if—you meet this man and form a relationship with him, you join in *his* circle. He remains at the center of the circle while you revolve around him, sliding comfortably into the supportive role that you learned early in life. You become *his* wife, *his* partner, *his* companion, *his* support, and the mother of *his* and your children.

The new circle, with our partner at the center, forms the basis of our Second Act. Work outside the home is usually less important than our lives within the circle. Or, in the case of a career to which we are devoted, it becomes the source of difficult conflicts, both within ourselves and between us and other family members. In addition, friendships, even those that are close and long term, often fall by the wayside. If you have children, the circle may shift, so that, at least for a time, they become the center. This may cause conflict within the circle, but one thing remains constant: You are not the center of the circle. *He* is, or the *children* are. But definitely not *you*.

This pattern may continue for many years. Although any particular circle may break down, we usually place the blame on our partner's incapacity to fill his role properly, ourselves for not choosing carefully, or other external, uncontrollable circumstances. Rarely do we think to blame the pattern itself. We simply look to replace our failed circle with a new one based on the same pattern but with a more capable person to maintain the center.

In the New Third Act, other people are no longer the center of our life, and our relationship with our partner becomes a wise teacher. Children leave, Prince Charming fades, time is short, and a new craving arises within us, urging us to reclaim our lives. We are the center of our own lives. At midlife the combination of external events and internal pressures forces us to make a choice: Will we cling to the old, outworn patterns and allow ourselves to decline into old age, or will we accept our new circumstances and create a new, fulfilling life in our New Third Act?

Some women cannot move into the New Third Act. Clinging to the old forms that shaped their Second Act, they struggle to re-create the picture as it looked then. They may marry again, and sometimes again, ostensibly looking for the "right" partner or doing what they think they should. They may intrude inappropriately into their children's lives. But that hardly ever works. Underneath, the shadow of desperation follows wherever they go. But aging is inevitable and offers a lesson in living. If we ignore it, deny it, or try to skip it, we end up on a downward spiral of confusion and depression. Our relationships stagnate. However, if we accept our new life with its invitation to grow, our life becomes more fulfilling and our relationships more vibrant and alive.

Now *you* become the central figure in the circle, larger than all the rest. The New Third Act is about you and your growth. That doesn't mean you will be alone. You may form a relationship that grows into a partnership, or you may continue the partnership you are already in, but the partner is no longer at the center of your circle. You are. He is in his own circle, and, if the relationship is healthy, your individual circles have a blissful merging point that doesn't overwhelm either of you. You are harmonious, equal partners.

Your partnership will be more satisfying than ever. Why is that true? Because both you and your partner will be grounded in yourself and engaged in a life that is fulfilling and satisfying. Rather than needing the other, you will be free to enjoy him as a friend and partner, walking the path of life in mutually supportive relationship with each other.

Moreover, whether or not you are in a partnership, your circle will not be empty. It will be filled with what fulfills *you:* your work, your passions, your dreams, your family, your friends, your home, and all that enriches *your* life. Just as when we were children, we will once again live from our core, our inner self, but this time that core is enriched by our years of experience and the wisdom of elderhood.

Friends

Friends can also be valuable teachers. This insight really hit home for me at a recent dinner with a dear friend. During our conversation, she made an observation about me that I normally would have shrugged off. She said, "Sue, I've been worried about you. You look so tired lately. I really care about you and want you to take care of yourself." Among women friends, such a comment is not unusual; we often say supportive things like that to each other. But that night I really *heard* it. I got that she really cared about me.

The comment stayed with me. Later that evening I found myself thinking, "Why did it take so long to sink in?" Then it dawned on me—that's a message I rarely heard from my own family. Neither of my parents was expressive when it came to feelings. Yet underneath, I always felt loved, so I excused their lack of communication, telling myself I didn't really need to hear it. But I did. We all do.

It's true that my mother frequently told me "Sue, you need to stand up for yourself" or "Sue, you always let other people take advantage of you." But I heard those comments as criticisms, not support. I didn't hear "I care about you." I heard "There's something wrong with you." And even later in life, when family members expressed concern for my health or well-being, it often seemed more about them than about me—"Take care of yourself, so you can be there for me." Unlike what I heard from my family, my friend's comment felt like true caring.

On further reflection, I asked myself, "Why did it sink in now, but never before?" Over the years, many people have expressed the concern that my friend expressed to me that night. Why didn't I hear them? I believe the answer is that I was not ready. Hearing the message and taking it in took preparation, gleaned from years of experience and self-reflection, for me to step outside of my "Mother complex" far enough to absorb new perspectives on myself. In other words, it probably could not have happened before I reached my New Third Act.

And here's the really interesting part: allowing myself to hear what my friend was saying not only changed my relationship with her, it changed my relationship to my mother as well—my mother who has been deceased for over twenty years. Impossible? Evidently not. That's because my relationship with my mother is something that I carry within myself, and when I change, it changes. Now, as I think back on my mother's words, I can hear them differently. On one level, she was indeed criticizing me, but on another, she was trying to help me. Her childhood experience had taught her that life was a survival contest, each woman for herself. If you didn't stand your ground or speak up, others would run over you. In other words, her motto was "Nice guys finish last." She had learned to do this, and it worked for her. She wanted the same for me. Pointing it out was her way of taking care of me. It was the best she knew how to do.

Whereas there are often pressures and obligations in choosing a partner and there is no choice involved with our family members, choosing friends offers the most personal choice of any of our close relationships. We can have a variety of friends in a variety of situations with some friends very close and others casual. Some friends are good relationships, but temporary for a number of reasons, whereas other friendships span our lifetimes. Friends can be trusted confidantes on their own or part of a treasured community.

The New Third Act, like relationships, is an inevitable part of life. How we live it is up to us. If we refuse to grow, we nevertheless get older and end up on a downward spiral feeling resentful, empty, and depressed. However, if we accept the challenge and allow ourselves to move fully into the new paradigm of the relationship circle, we discover our power and wisdom, and feel the joy of the crowning moment of our lives. Our relationships reflect this crowning moment.

 Reflect:

What patterns formed through family have you shifted? How did you do this? From this lesson, what is another pattern you want to work on?

Have you reclaimed the center of your "circle story" in your partnership? Have you found a blissful merging point with your existing partner, or how do you envision this in a new partnership?

What was a special gift of growth you received through a friendship? What did this teach you? How do you share this lesson with your friends?

23
Finding Your True Work

We usually think of "work" as performing tasks around the home, office, or community, having a job or career, or filling our lives with some of both. But more than that, each of us has within ourselves a unique pattern of talents and strengths that are unlike those of others, and anyone of us can, and should, utilize it for friends and family, as well as for the benefit of society. That is finding our true work.

I understand that many Native Americans consider "work" their "Personal Medicine." They believe that our purpose in life is to identify our Personal Medicine and share it with the world for the benefit of all. I love this idea, but I also know that developing our Personal Medicine—or our work—is not brief or easy. For most of us, it takes time, sometimes years, of working on our inner selves and developing a spiritual base from which to draw our strengths. We also need the courage to persist and overcome obstacles that block our paths, and discover and cultivate well-honed skills that enable us to express our Personal Medicine effectively.

Finding our true work is important in every stage of our life, but it is especially important in the New Third Act. It is then the external responsibilities we carried in our Second Act fade to the background, and our personal life comes to the forefront. By then we have the experience and wisdom to utilize our work in the fullest sense.

The Path to My Personal Medicine

For me, it definitely took time. After years of searching and bouncing from one career to another—music teacher, junior high school counselor, college professor—I finally found the career that felt right in my early fifties, the one that I knew was my true work: counseling and therapy. In the years since then, drawn by my own interests and by the needs of the clients who presented themselves to me, I increasingly focused on the lives of women, especially those in the Third Act. Working with these women has brought me a deeper sense of satisfaction than I had ever previously experienced. I felt I was finally doing the work I was meant to do. I had found my Personal Medicine.

I recall the early beginning of this path when I was a young child, maybe three years old. I was sitting with my mother on the front porch steps, relishing the time alone with her. It didn't happen often, and I loved the times it did. That day my brother and father were both gone—my brother was playing ball with friends at the local ball field and my father was still working at the Kroger store he managed. So, I had my mother all to myself, at least for a little while.

We talked, and though I don't remember what we said, I began to wonder what she thinks about things. So I asked, "Mommy, what's it like to be you?" I really wanted to know, and I thought she would tell me, but instead, she just laughed a little and went on to something else. I was disappointed because I really wanted to find out what it was like to be her. Over the years, this was a problem for me. I wanted to know what it was like to be another person, and also to find out if I was as good as other people. I really didn't trust that I was okay. Yet within this doubt was the seed that I had strong feelings about this.

I know that my mother did not purposely mean to disappoint me. She probably thought that what I said was cute, but not important. Looking back on it, I asked myself, how would things be different if my mother had treated my question as important? Would I feel like I was important, and if so, how was I important? Would I be like my brother, that is, a smart kid with a good brain that could be encouraged to grow and do something very special? What would be different if my mother saw my question as an example of intelligence and caring, and if she had said, "You're just as smart as your brother, but in a different kind of way; he has strengths, but so do you. Your strengths are important because they include how you notice other people and care about them."

As it turned out, over the years I came to realize those things and—as you may have guessed—that was what led me into becoming a therapist. My intuition guided me through my interest and excitement in choosing intellectual exploration that brought both new ideas and more questions. I recognized my enjoyment in the process, how easy it came, as well as how it energized me. These feelings multiplied as I went on to personal interactions. Here, I added more answers and more questions as other people—some therapists, some friends—shared life stories and observations about me for encouragement. I noticed how much I admired them for their compassionate honesty and inspiration, and I wanted to develop those gifts within myself. This recognition and gratitude for sharing of *their* gifts led me to recognize my *own* feminine powers. Using these, I have continued to nurture a circle of growth for others, and through reflection on this work, I have grown more myself. Therefore, I feel admiration for those women I work with.

I also admire my mother all the more as I acknowledge the ideal path my life has taken. Her comparing me to my brother may have hindered me. And perhaps even her recognition of my strengths would have denied me the self-exploration that, through my own work, has been a glorious discovery and cherished gift to live my life with. My mother did her best from her power and strengths, and I thank her for it. I am grateful for my path and discovery of my own Personal Medicine and having the opportunity to share it with clients, friends, family, and now other women that I may never meet, but with whom I am honored to have connection.

Discovering Your Personal Medicine

There is no one right way to identifying your unique pattern of strengths and power to fulfilling the promise of your Personal Medicine. Just as your Personal Medicine is unique to you, so is the path to achieving it. Basically, this is a matter of finding what *feels* right and what you *know* in your bones is right for you. When that happens, you have found your Personal Medicine.

If you need help getting started, consider your answers to the reflective questions throughout the book. You may take hints from what I shared above, too. Also, consider recognizing and speaking with a woman—or several—in her New Third Act who loves her work. Ask her about the process she took to reach fulfillment. This may assist you in gaining insight and inspiration.

Also, you may follow the questions below. Ask yourself what each one means to you—perhaps as far back as early childhood—and how it affected, or still affects, your life. Then look for what you can do to change or improve it.

What comes easy for you? Often, we discount what we do easily, just because it is so easy—"Oh, that was nothing!" But the fact is that it is easy because it's one of your strengths. Others may admire you for it and find it very difficult to do themselves. So, instead of discounting these qualities, find ways to develop and offer them.

What do you enjoy? We often believe if it's fun, it can't be worthwhile. Not so. If it's fun, it probably means we're in our flow, and that's where we want to be. The question is, how do you develop that "fun" activity into something really worthwhile?

What gives you energy? Some activities may invigorate you. Notice when you have finished, do you feel energized, or maybe tired, but not drained? If so, that activity is probably one of your strengths and can lead you to your Personal Medicine.

What do you have strong feelings about? Feelings are messengers from our soul, so pay attention. When we're in our flow, it *feels* right; when we veer off that path, we *know* something is wrong. We can express our full power only when we are true to ourselves.

What does your intuition tell you? You may think that you're not intuitive, but that's not true. We're all intuitive, although we may experience it in different ways. It may come as a "gut feeling," a sudden "knowing," an image or vision, a body sensation, a dream, or many other ways. Tune in to your intuition; your spirit is speaking to you.

What do you admire in others? The strengths you admire in others may be your own denied strengths that you project onto them. Look closely and identify the qualities you admire in these people, and ask yourself if these qualities could be part of you. Practice living them, and see what happens.

What were you good at when you were a child? As children, we were freer to be who we were; in fact, we didn't know how to be any other way. So taking a look at the past may give you a clue about your natural abilities, now hidden under layers of socialization. How can you transform your childhood talents into adult strengths and your true work?

What did your family criticize or fail to notice about you? Parents often don't see their children's strengths, or they do see them but label them as negative qualities. This happens most often to children who are very different from their parents, or whose strengths threaten or challenge their parents in some way. You may grow up not knowing your strengths, or worse, believing that they were somehow "bad."

What are your feminine powers? Remember that as a woman, your strengths may be discounted or demeaned. That doesn't mean they aren't strengths. The capacity to *feel, intuit, nurture,* and *empathize* are women's strengths that our society needs.

Using Your Personal Medicine

Notice if your answers to the Personal Medicine questions illuminated certain patterns and paths. Perhaps ideas for developing these strengths and talents, then taking them out into the world is becoming clearer. Imagine how you can create your true work from these insights. And give it a try while staying aware to adapt further to find the most ideal way to demonstrate your Personal Medicine successfully.

Epilogue

The Call of This Moment to Be Real

Becoming real takes time.

For my growth as a woman, I discovered that a significant portion of my Personal Medicine was to write and publish a book. This happened quite unexpectedly around my 70th birthday.

Over the years, I went through all the impatience, handwringing, revision after revision, and draft after draft until I completed this book. To reach my writing goal took over a decade. Clearly this accomplishment covered about fifteen percent of my lifetime. Seems like a while until it's compared to the time spent in marriage, raising children, caretaking of family members, building a career then building another one. . .and another one.

Interestingly enough, though, it's the same length of time I spent living my childhood before knowing that the First Act even led to a Second Act, much less a third one. And nowhere on my little radar was the wonderful idea of a *New* Third Act.

Yet from about the time around age 60 when my therapist announced, "Your whole life sounds like an accident!" the impressions and indicators were coming into my awareness. The world was changing, but I was so wrapped up in my accidental life, trying to get to a place where everything was "okay," that I didn't recognize that the world was *always* changing. Eventually, I figured out that I could choose to change myself and live an intentional life. Better yet, I could start now.

Plenty in life happens unexpectedly, but it's how we receive it, the way we view it, and what we choose to do with it that forms our intentions moment to moment. And whether we notice them or not, these moments build—into years, careers, grown children, major anniversaries, decades—into a lifetime.

As a woman at the pinnacle of your life, you have the opportunity and the empowered choice to recognize the life you're living right now. And if you discover you're living a fantasy—whether your own or one of someone

The Call of This Moment to Be Real

else's making—you can choose to step into reality and change. Now—right now—you can choose to be real.

I have, and over the years it has often brought me joy and peace in bigger ways than I've ever known. Some bigger than I could imagine.

So to you, my friend, I send my heartfelt invitation to join me in the New Third Act.

Becoming real *does* take time, yet it can happen at *any* time. It's never, ever too late.

And really, now *is* the perfect time.

Acknowledgements

Writing this book has been a journey of discovery unlike any other in my life. Adding a facet to both personal experience and growing knowledge, this book is a crystal clear reflection over a career and life well lived and deeply loved. Through this, so many people have shared, listened, contributed, and supported me, and I thank them with all my heart.

I thank my husband of 47 years, Tim Carr, for his unwavering support through all my endeavors. Tim, we have been a team of individuals with distinct skills, always encouraging one another to grow on our desired paths as we share our journey as partners. I'm grateful for your enthusiastic knowledge of systems and order, how you embraced the computer age and allowed me to benefit from your masterful skills. Mostly, I'm grateful for our cherished love and growth.

My gratitude to my sons Chris and John, daughter-in-law Paula, grandchildren Sara and Hunter, and my brother Dick. Family is both the beginning of and the constant companion in personal growth. I'm grateful to all my family for their continuous loving support.

To my writing coach, editor, and friend Wayne South Smith, for encouraging me to take a class on journaling, and within this, recognizing that the materials I developed for workshops could be a book. My desire ignited. Through the years and pages of writing, you never let my passion wither. You have challenged me by presenting new ideas and ways to express myself in writing, as well as given me encouragement to persevere.

To my graphic designer, photographer, and friend Laura Nalesnik. You have captured the essence of my work in beautiful imagery, and these designs have proudly served as the symbols for my practice and workshops for over a decade. You've also brought a lot of joyous color into my life.

To my friends—Lalor, Trisha, Laura H., Lynn, Mary, Emi, Jean N., Ann, Ellen, Laura N., George and Ruth, as well as Ardath and Beth, friends no longer at my side—from the time we met, there has been strong connection and solid bonding. The support from true friends is unique and a treasure.

Acknowledgements

I am also very grateful to my mentors Jean H. and Kathy M. for their guidance both professional and personal.

I thank my clients from the beginning of my practice, especially those women 50 and up. When I began my work as a therapist, I was just entering my Third Act. I leapt from the typical therapeutic/educational aspect in my work, from sessions with a pad and pen between us coupled with a non-reactive observant attitude, to fully receiving and feeling your words and emotions, even reflecting it upon my own life. You encouraged great humility and sisterhood as we both experienced simultaneous healing. As I began to write materials for workshops, these women then showed me what it's like to live at that age, and through our interactions, they guided me into the life that my work became about.

To all those women who came to me for counseling and group work as my practice grew and focused on women in the Third Act, you were the spark that lit the idea to share the discoveries both professionally and personally with a broader audience. I was both facilitator and participant, and that aspect of feminine companionship was both healing and inspiring, the core of my work over the past 30 years. I truly learned something through every single interaction as we grew together.

And finally, I want to thank my mother and my father. They provided inspiration for this book by living life the best ways they knew how, and by allowing me to recognize this in them and, eventually, in myself.

About The Author

During a 30-year career as a clinical psychologist in private practice, Suzanne Justice Carr's passion has guided women in midlife. In addition to individual counseling, Suzanne has created and led empowerment groups and retreats on The New Third Act, Crone Wisdom, and Wise Women, among other topics.

Her seminars and presentations have served audiences for the American Psychological Association, the Georgia Psychological Association, the Association of Women in Psychology, Atlanta Women in Business, Jewish Family and Career Services, Emory Center for Lifelong Learning, Millennium Health Care, and Summit Ridge Hospital, among others.

Prior to her clinical practice, she served a combined ten years as an Associate Professor at Atlanta's Spelman College and an instructor at Clark College after working ten years in the public school system in Florida as a counselor and teacher of secondary education.

Her PhD from Georgia State University in Social/Developmental Psychology with certification in Clinical Psychology follows a Masters in Guidance and Counseling from the University of Florida, Gainesville, and a Bachelor of Arts, Cum Laude, from Radcliffe College in Cambridge, Massachusetts.

She lives in Atlanta with Tim, her husband of 47 years and close to her sons, John and Chris, as well as extended family and friends. She can be reached at suzanne.carr@mindspring.com.

Made in the USA
Lexington, KY
10 April 2015